CONTROVERSIES IN LAW AND SPORT

Curtis Fogel

CONTROVERSIES IN LAW AND SPORT

Curtis Fogel

COMMON GROUND RESEARCH NETWORKS 2017

First published in 2017
as part of the Sport & Society Book Imprint
doi:10.18848/978-1-61229-905-1/CGP (Full Book)

Common Ground Research Networks
2001 South First Street, Suite 202
University of Illinois Research Park
Champaign, IL 61820

Copyright © Curtis Fogel 2017

All rights reserved. Apart from fair dealing for the purposes of study, research, criticism or review as permitted under the applicable copyright legislation, no part of this book may be reproduced by any process without written permission from the publisher.

Library of Congress Cataloging-in-Publication Data

Names: Fogel, Curtis, 1983- author.
Title: Controversies in law and sport / Curtis Fogel.
Description: Champaign, IL : Common Ground Research Networks, 2017. |
  Includes bibliographical references and index.
Identifiers: LCCN 2016026208 (print) | LCCN 2016030535 (ebook) | ISBN
  9781612299051 (pdf) | ISBN 9781612299037 (hbk : alk. paper) | ISBN
  9781612299044 (pbk : alk. paper)
Subjects: LCSH: Sports--Law and legislation.
Classification: LCC K3702 (ebook) | LCC K3702 .F64 2017 (print) | DDC
  344/.099--dc23
LC record available at https://lccn.loc.gov/2016026208

Cover Photo Credit: Mimi Dokken

Table of Contents

Acknowledgements ix

Chapter 1 1
Clashes of Law and Sport

Chapter 2 9
On Privileged Grounds: Sport Specificity and the Law

Chapter 3 17
Policing Femininity: Intersex Discrimination in International Athletics

Chapter 4 29
Breaking Uneven: Legal and Competitive Issues of UEFA's Financial Fair Play Regulations

Chapter 5 39
Bloodsport: Violence and Criminal Law in British Rugby

Chapter 6 59
Million-Dollar Amateurs: NCAA Sport, Student-Athlete Image, Rights, and Anti-Trust Law

Chapter 7 67
Illegal Muscle: Legal Issues in Doping Control

Chapter 8 77
Pay-to-Play: Online Fantasy Sports, Gambling, and the Law

Chapter 9 85
Sports in the Courts and the Rise of Alternative Dispute Resolution:
A Critical Analysis of Sport Dispute Resolution Mechanisms

Chapter 10 95
Future Directions in Sports Law, Regulation, and Dispute Resolution

References 103

List of Acronyms 125

Legal Case Index 127

ACKNOWLEDGEMENTS

This book was written over many years and with institutional support from four university departments in three different countries that I have been affiliated with, which has shaped its international scope, including the Faculty of Law at De Montfort University in Leicester, England; the Canadian Studies Program at University of California, Berkeley in the United States; the Criminology Program at Lakehead University Orillia in Canada; and the Department of Sport Management at Brock University in St. Catharines, Canada. I am very much indebted to the students I have taught over the last eight years in classes on Sports Law, Social Problems in Sports, Sociology of Sport, and Sports Ethics, who have enthusiastically and critically engaged with the ideas and arguments throughout this book. I would especially like to thank those who have read and commented on the manuscript, or chapters therein, including Vaughan Hall, Neil Parpworth, Michael Rohatynsky, Andy Gray, Jonathon Merritt, Vanessa Bettinson, Andrea Quinlan, Chris Morriss-Roberts, and Jorg Krieger. I am indebted to everyone at Common Ground Research Networks, and McCall Macomber in particular, who has contributed to the publication process, as well as Mimi Dokken for so generously allowing the use of her photograph on the cover.

CHAPTER 1

Clashes of Law and Sport

INTRODUCTION

Sport and the law are generally considered to be separate and distinct social institutions. On occasion, however, they collide: a hockey player deliberately strikes his stick into the face of an opponent (Barnes, 2010); a female sprinter is accused of having masculine characteristics and is required to withdraw from competition (Camporesi & Maugeri, 2016); a student-athlete who generates millions of dollars in revenue for his university is suspended for accepting money to sign an autograph (McMurphy, 2016); an Olympic skeleton racer uses a hair regrowth medicine on the World-Anti-Doping Agency (WADA) banned list and is disqualified from Winter Olympic competition (Abrahamson, 2006). This book examines these and other controversial issues in international sports, both on and off the field, and explores the often complicated and complex clashes between law and sport.

As the sports industry grows, so too does the significance of law in regulating sport and its commercial aspects. This book is not a how-to guide for sports lawyers or managers seeking step-by-step guidance for remedying sport disputes, writing or challenging player contracts, or detailing all potential legal issues in sport. Instead, the primary aim of the book is to critically explore several controversial legal issues in national and international sport and examine how the controversies have arisen, detail the complications presented by competing regulations within law and sport, and make recommendations for effectively addressing the conflicts in ways that are lawful and beneficial to athletes, sport managers, team owners, spectators, and others involved in the sports industry.

What Is Sport?

There is much debate in academic literatures in Sociology, Philosophy, Kinesiology, and Sport Studies on how to define sport. Literary theorists have also mused on the topic of "What is sport?" and have contemplated its central characteristics and explored its boundaries (see Barnes, 2007). While many activities appear to have widespread acceptance as sports (e.g. ice hockey), others are somewhat debatable (e.g. chess). For the purposes of this book, sport is understood as having several key characteristics, which are detailed below.

According to Coakley and Donnelly (2004, 2009), sports are oriented around competition and goal attainment, where evaluative mechanisms such as times and scores are used to determine athletic performance results. Competitive goal attainment can be in the form of winning games, tournaments, or league championships. It can also relate to personal goals, such as finishing in the top 20 of a running event, or finishing a race in a specific time. In sports, there is a winner and participants/teams are ranked in descending order based on their performance. Without this competitive element, physical activity can be more accurately labeled as play or recreational activity.

Sports include some form of physical exertion, dexterity, and specialized training of the mind and body for competition. The primary competitor must be a human, although animals can also be involved if their activity is connected to human activity, e.g. horse-racing, as well as motorized vehicles, e.g. motor sports. If no human skill is directly involved in the competitive act, then it is arguably not a sport, e.g. greyhound racing. Sports have athletes who engage in specialized training, often using specialized equipment, to increase their physical and cognitive abilities to succeed in competitions and attain goals such as winning.

Sports also have specified rules, traditions, and governance structures that organize competitions and events. Without a recognized governing body or federation with established and widely accepted rules, an activity cannot be considered to be a sport. For an activity to be included in the Summer or Winter Olympics, for example, it must have an International Federation (IF) and the IF rules and regulations must conform to the Olympic Charter including adherence to the World Anti-Doping Agency Code. Not all sports are included in the Olympics (e.g. American gridiron football), as other criteria are also used to determine Olympic acceptability not related to sport definitions, but the most widely recognized international sports are included in the Olympics. And, even those sports that are not in the Olympics have governing bodies with clear and well-established rules.

In summary, sports are competitive activities, governed by organizations with well-established rules and regulations, which involve specialized training and equipment to enhance the mind and body in pursuit of goals and achievements. Defining sport is not only important for a better understanding of the content of this book, it is also an important discussion to the exploration of controversies in sport and law.

What is and is not a sport has legal implications. For example, can a legal dispute between a chess player and the World Chess Federation (FIDE) be taken to the Court of Arbitration for Sport (CAS)? Likewise, do chess players have a "right to sport" under Article 1 of the International Charter on Physical Education and Sport (1978) (ICPES) declaration that:

> Every human being has a fundamental right of access to physical education and sport ... [and the] ... freedom to develop physical, intellectual and moral powers through physical education and sport must be guaranteed both within the educational system and in other aspects of social life.

In the case of chess, the answer is likely yes as, although the physical exertion element is somewhat questionable, the other characteristics are in place including an international federation that defines itself as a sport, and a recent partnership with WADA to develop a prohibited list of performance-enhancing drugs for chess players

(FIDE, 2015). To provide a contrast, Monopoly players would likely have a much harder time arguing for a human right to play Monopoly, or to appeal to CAS for sport-related arbitration services, as Monopoly does not have the characteristics common to all sports.

The Significance of Sport

The social institution of sport has tremendous economic, social, political, and cultural significance worldwide. Not all countries cherish the same sports and participate in all sports, but all countries worldwide engage in organized sporting events. According to Burstyn (1999),

> The rituals of sport engage more people in a shared experience than any other institution or cultural activity today. World Cup soccer gathers upwards of a billion electronic spectators on a global basis. According to generally accepted estimates, between two billion and three billion people—close to half of the humans on this planet—followed the 1996 Atlanta Olympic Games on television or radio (p. 3).

According to LaVoi and Kane (2011), "sport influences almost every aspect of our lives" (p. 374).

Economically, sport has become increasingly corporatized and commercialized on a national and global scale. A single thirty-second commercial advertisement during the 2016 Superbowl of the National Football League (NFL) cost upwards of $5 million, or roughly $170,000 per second of advertising (Woodyard, 2016). In 2014, the NFL reported league revenues of approximately $11 billion USD (Kaplan, 2015), Major League Baseball (MLB) reported revenues amounting to approximately $9 billion (Brown, 2014), and the National Basketball Association (NBA) $5 billion (Badenhausen, 2014). That is a combined reported revenue of over $25 billion for just three American professional sports leagues.

Sport participation is common in most peoples' lives worldwide. A 2006 survey of over two thousand International Federation of Association Football (FIFA) member associations worldwide indicated that 270 million people currently participate in football, or what is commonly termed soccer in North America (Kuntz, 2006). The National Federation of State High School Associations (NFHS) in the United States reported that 7,807,047 high school students participated in an organized high school sport in 2015 (NFHS, 2015).

Whether as a participant, fan, organizer, local business owner, athlete supporter, or CEO of a supranational corporation, sport impacts peoples' lives worldwide. It has the potential to be very beneficial through promoting health and well-being, teaching discipline and positive values, generating community revenue, and bringing people together with shared goals and interests. It also has the potential to be damaging and destructive, leading to severe injuries, conflict, controversies, and disputes. Law is one potential remedy to help ensure the positive aspects of sport can flourish, while minimizing the potentially damaging consequences of organized sport in capitalist societies.

The Significance of Law in Sport and the Emergence of Sports Law

As is the case in society more generally, legal regulation and litigation have become a common reality in modern sport. This has been referred to as "the juridification of sport" (Gardiner & Felix, 1995, p. 189). The law provides guidance, values, mechanisms, and structures that can contribute to the successful functioning and management of sport. However, despite increased case law and legal scholarship on the topic of law and sport, the precise role of law in the regulation of sport remains unclear and controversial, with questions arising about when, how, and why the courts should become involved in sporting matters, and when, how, and why sports organizations should be permitted to maintain "the autonomy of sport" with the right to govern themselves free of interference and influence of law, politics, and private commercial influence (Geeraert & Mrkonjic, 2014, p. 473). There are complex and ongoing interactions between the rules of law and rules of sport that create a largely undefined and evolving regulatory structure in sport at all levels and in all jurisdictions.

It is often argued that no specific field of law actually exists that can be termed Sports Law (Donnellan, 2010; Grayson, 1999). Law and sport come into contact through several distinct areas of law such as human rights, contracts, competition law, privacy law, criminal law, civil/tort law, labour/employment law, competition/anti-trust law, intellectual property, administrative law, and so forth. Sports law is concerned with how different distinct areas of law can be and are applied to problems, disputes, and issues in the context of sport. Furthermore, unlike distinct areas of law, sports law does not have an identifiable body of law from which it is derived. For example, criminal law is derived in large part from criminal codes in particular jurisdictions. It can then be argued that sports law is not really a distinct field of law, but rather the application of distinct fields of law to a particular context, prompting the common use of the phrase "law and sport" rather than sports law.

Some scholars have argued that a distinct field of sports law, or what some term Lex Sportiva, does in fact exist (Beloff, 2012; McLaren, 2001). Lewis and Taylor (2003) suggest that sports law is a new, distinct field of law that is emerging as sports-related case law continues to grow, as do the capacities of CAS. Likewise, Barnes (1996) contends that distinct legal doctrine exists through the proliferation of sports legislation, litigation, and arbitral decisions. Barnes (1996) provides an early, and comprehensive, definition of the distinct field of sports law as follows:

> Sports law addresses basic ethical issues of freedom, fairness, equality, safety and economic security. The subject matter of sports law includes State control and subsidy of sport, rights of access, disciplinary powers and procedures, commercial and property rights, employment relations and compensation for injuries. Sports law is grounded in the material dimensions

of sport and includes a study of the life and times of its heroic practitioners. (p. 2)

For Barnes (1996), and others, the field of sports law is largely a given, and in time will continue to grow into a more recognizable field of legal practice, research, and theorizing.

Whether or not the term sports law, law and sport, or lex sportiva are used to describe the field, there is an undeniable significance of law in the regulation of all aspects of contemporary sports. The aim of this book is to contribute to this growing area of legal practice and academic inquiry by exploring controversies that can arise and have arisen in the intersections of sport and law. In doing so, this book offers recommendations for preventing and resolving many problems and disputes that interfere with the safe, fair, and virtuous functioning of sport.

Organization of the Book

Chapter two, titled "On Privileged Grounds: Sport Specificity and the Law," examines the extent to which sport is, and should be, considered special and unique in the eyes of the law to warrant specific legal exemptions. It examines different areas of law as they relate to sport, including 1) administrative law, 2) privacy law, 3) human rights law, 4) labour and employment law, 5) criminal law, and 6) EU law. Through this analysis, the chapter argues that while no all-encompassing exception from the law exists in sport, sport does receive special considerations and privileges that are often necessary to preserve the integrity, fairness, commercial interests, and traditions of sports.

Chapter three, titled "Policing Femininity: Intersex Discrimination in International Athletics," examines the practice of sex testing in international athletics and explores potential legal challenges to sex testing on the grounds of discrimination under human rights law. Since their inclusion in the 1928 Olympics, female athletes have had to undergo different tests from "nude parades," to chromosome assessment, to DNA analysis to police their femininity in sport. Female athletes deemed to have intersex or biologically masculine characteristics have been banned from competition or required to undergo treatment such as hormone therapy. This has been a highly controversial—and potentially unlawful—practice, particularly since male athletes do not go through similar tests.

Chapter four, titled "Breaking Uneven: Legal and Competitive Issues of UEFA's Financial Fair Play Regulations," examines the legality and fairness of new Financial Fair Play (FFP) regulations that have been created by the Union of European Football Associations (UEFA) to reduce club overspending and promote long-term financial sustainability. Unlike salary cap regulations used in North America that restrict sports teams to maximum expenditures, FFP regulations allow clubs that make more money to spend more, while teams that make less money are required to spend less, with the goal that all teams break even at season's end at the very least. The outcome is, however, that competitive imbalance arises that could be deemed unlawful on various grounds in EU Law.

Chapter five, titled "Bloodsport: Violence and Criminal Law in British Rugby," examines the unclear threshold between sports violence and criminal violence in the context of British rugby. Twenty-one criminal prosecutions in the UK for alleged thuggery on the pitch are examined, and the unique challenges of prosecuting rugby violence are identified, including issues related to unclear laws, establishing actus reus and mens rea, discerning consent, and maintaining public interests. Arguments and specifications for the establishment of a clear, research-informed, and balanced sports-violence criminalization threshold test are presented.

Chapter six, titled "Million-Dollar Amateurs: NCAA Sport, Student-Athlete Image Rights, and Anti-Trust Law," examines the legality of the National Collegiate Athletics Association's (NCAA) longstanding policy of amateurism that hold that despite the billions of dollars in revenue that collegiate football and basketball players generate in the United States that they can only be compensated with scholarships that cover education-related expenses. The chapter focuses specifically on the cases of *O'Bannon* (2010/2014), *Hart* (2013), and *Keller* (2010) who originally filed separate lawsuits alleging anti-trust and right of publicity violations after their personas were used in Electronic Arts (EA) video games without receiving compensation.

Chapter seven, titled "Illegal Muscle: Legal Issues in Doping Control," examines the legality, fairness, and effectiveness of current WADA doping control policies and strategies. The chapter argues that an effective strategy for the prevention of doping in sport should rest on harm reduction principles of educating athletes about the potential harms of drug use, teaching safe alternatives to achieving their athletic goals to reduce demand, and targeting traffickers of prohibited substances rather than restricting the rights and freedoms of athletes with ineffective results.

Chapter eight, titled "Pay-to-Play: Online Fantasy Sports, Gambling, and the Law," examines the legal aspects of online fantasy sports as a potential form of gambling and looks specifically at gambling laws and legislation in the United States. Online fantasy sports are a multi-billion dollar industry in the United States, and yet the laws pertaining to the industry remain somewhat unclear and undecided. In *Humphrey* and *Langone*, the respective courts ruled that fantasy sports do not constitute illegal gambling. Differences in state gambling laws have, however, kept some uncertainty over the legality of fantasy sports in some states where fantasy sports providers have restricted participant access to pay-for-play fantasy competitions.

Chapter nine, titled "Sports in the Courts and the Rise of Alternative Dispute Resolution: A Critical Analysis of Sports Dispute Resolution Mechanisms," examines the potential shortcomings of an over-reliance on the courts to address sporting disputes, and critically explores the benefits and drawbacks of three main forms of Alternative Dispute Resolution (ADR) including negotiation, mediation, and arbitration. This chapter argues that ADR can provide certain advantages over litigation in many cases by reducing costs, building problem-solving capacity, maintaining good working and business relationships, ensuring privacy and confidentiality, and allowing for quick and flexible processes and decisions, while ensuring that independent experts in both sport and law are aiding in dispute resolution.

Chapter 10, titled "Future Directions in Sports Law, Regulation, and Dispute Resolution," concludes the book with a brief look at future legal issues and challenges that will likely by faced in the context of sport, and critically assesses seven different strategies to resolve sports problems and disputes including 1) increased formal social control, 2) self-regulation, 3) balanced legal reform, 4) establishing separate national laws on sport, 5) creation and expansion of independent sports violence tribunals, 6) reorienting sport, and 7) furthering the development of sports law as a distinct and established legal field.

CHAPTER 2

On Privileged Grounds: Sport Specificity and the Law

Introduction

Agamben (2005) describes a "state of exception" as a jurisdiction in which laws have been suspended for a specified purpose, typically to maintain order and security in times of emergency, such as wartime crisis. In a state of exception laws of a particular nation are replaced with laws more suitable to the particular conditions that are being faced. It does not mean that there are no laws. Instead, the regular laws are suspended and replaced by different laws. The central question examined in this chapter is: does a state of legal exception exist in the context of sport and sporting competitions?

Many terms are commonly used to refer to the notion that sport might exist in a state of exception, such as *sporting exemption, sport monopoly, specialness of sport,* and *autonomy of sport*. The most common term that has emerged more recently in sports studies and law literature, largely because of its use in the White Paper on Sport (2007), is the term *specificity of sport* or *sport specificity*. The basic notion behind these terms is the belief that (i) sport has an inherent uniqueness or specialness to it, and (ii) that due to this uniqueness/specialness, sport should have exemptions from law.

There can be little debate that sport specificity has been established through various pieces of legislation and legal proceedings. The question is: to what extent does the specificity of sport exist? Is sport in a full state of exception where sport administrators have totalitarian rule over matters that occur on fields of play, or is it much less autonomous than that? Through an examination of different areas of law, it is argued in this chapter that no all-encompassing exception from the law exists in sport, but that sport does receive special considerations and privileges allowing for many exemptions from the law. Furthermore, it is argued that some legal exemptions are necessary to preserve the integrity, fairness, commercial interests, and traditions of sports.

Conflicts Between Legislation, Law, and Sport

The legislation of paramount importance to establishing the potential for sports exemptions from the law include, but are not limited to: 1) Declaration on Sport in the Treaty of Amsterdam (1997), 2) Helsinki Report on Sport (1999), 3) Declaration on Sport in the Treaty of Nice (2000), 4) White Paper on Sport (2007), 5) Treaty on the Functioning of the European Union (TFEU, 2009), and 6) UN Resolution on the Autonomy of Sport (2014). A commonality in these documents is that a unique specialness of sport is recognized that opens the possibility for particular exceptions to law in the self-governance of sport, combined with an assertion that no absolute exceptions from law shall be granted. This assertion is summarized well in Article 165 of the TFEU, which states, "The Union shall contribute to the promotion of European sporting issues, while taking account of the specific nature of sport."

Through case law, the existence and limits of the exceptions in sport can be further identified and clarified. For the purposes of this chapter, six areas of law will be explored where clashes between sport and law are commonplace, looking specifically at how questions of possible exceptions have been handled in courts of law. The legal areas explored include: 1) administrative law, 2) privacy law, 3) human rights law, 4) labour and employment law, 5) criminal law, and 6) EU law.

Sport and Administrative Law

When appeals of disciplinary hearings in sport have reached the courts, a repeated assertion has been made by the courts that for rulings of governing bodies of sport to stand, maintaining the autonomy of sport, they must abide by the principles of natural justice. This means that while governing bodies in sport might have some freedom to hold disciplinary hearings and govern themselves, it is not without legal oversight from the courts. As such, the procedures followed in sports governance and disciplinary proceedings do not appear to exist in a state of exception.

Many cases have established and reinforced this precedent that governing bodies of sport must abide by these principles. For example, the judge presiding over *Enderby Town FC v. The Football Association* (1971)[1] stated: "The long and the short of it is that if the court sees that a domestic tribunal is proposing to proceed in a manner contrary to natural justice, it can intervene to stop it." Likewise, in *Jones v. Welsh Rugby Football Union* (1997),[2] the judge stated:

> It was an implied term of their contracts that in matters of discipline the Union would (a) properly apply its own rules and procedures in such a way as to produce a fair disciplinary process and (b) conduct those disciplinary procedures fairly, reasonably and in accordance with the rules of natural justice.

Similarly, in *Irvine v. Royal Burgess Golfing Society of Edinburgh* (2004), Yuill Irvine was suspended from a golf club for 12 months for wearing "ordinary" shoes on the course and other behaviours deemed unacceptable by the club management. He successfully challenged the ruling in court on the basis that the rules of natural justice were not followed and had his membership reinstated.

In relation to doping control in sport, it might be argued that some exemptions do exist in the way that governing bodies of sport handle such matters. CAS has

---

[1] Enderby Town FC brought forward the case when they were denied by the Football Association from being able to have legal representation at an appeal hearing over a fine they received.
[2] Mark Jones was suspended by a disciplinary review panel of the Welsh Rugby Football Union. He brought forward a complaint that the disciplinary review panel failed to follow the principles of natural justice.

established that the use of prohibited substances in sport is a strict liability offence. This means that positive drug test results are taken to be an indication of guilt. It is no longer possible for athletes to argue on the basis of inadvertent drug use that they should not be held responsible for the presence of banned substances in their bodies. The most famous example of this predating the CAS ruling would be from the 1988 Olympics where Canadian sprinter Ben Johnson's initial defence was that he had unknowingly ingested steroids on route to winning the gold medal. While he was unsuccessful in his defence, American sprinter Carl Lewis used the same argument of inadvertent use and successfully had his silver medal upgraded to the gold medal that Johnson was required to give back (Johnson & Moore, 1988).

Such defences are no longer valid under current anti-doping standards. As such, it can be argued that the principles of natural justice and the right to a defence thereof have been ignored in sport and that the courts are allowing a special exception. However, disciplinary hearings still occur in cases of doping offences whereby the athlete could present a defence that challenges the merit of the test results. Furthermore, strict liability offences are not uncommon outside the context of sport, especially in relation to regulatory offences e.g. a speeding ticket.

Sport and Privacy Law

Another possible legal exception for sport is additional freedoms to encroach on the privacy rights of athletes and spectators. While there are many areas where this could be explored, two will be examined here including public undress and drug testing.

As will be discussed in Chapter 3, female athletes have long been required to undergo medical examinations of their genital organs to determine if they are biologically female. This practice has not been legally challenged, so it is difficult to say for certain that any privacy exemption has been granted to allow for this invasion of privacy. However, United States courts have faced challenges in youth sport on the grounds of privacy rights of young athletes being violated, for which the courts have granted sport some additional leeway indicating that athletes are granted less privacy expectations than non-athletes. In *Vernonia School District 47J v. Acton* (1995),[3] the United States Supreme Court ruled that:

> Legitimate privacy expectations are even less with regard to student athletes. School sports are not for the bashful. They require "suiting up" before each practice or event, and showering and changing afterwards. Public school locker rooms, the usual sites for these activities, are not notable for the privacy they afford... No individual dressing rooms are provided; showerheads are lined up along a wall, unseparated by any sort of partition or curtain; not even all the toilet stalls have doors. As the United States Court of Appeals for the Seventh Circuit has noted, there is "an element of 'communal undress' inherent in athletic participation." (p. 657)

---

[3] The lawfulness of random drug tests of high school student-athletes in Virginia was challenged.

As such, some exception to basic standards of privacy appears to be granted to sport in the United States.

This is a similar issue in relation to performance-enhancing drug testing in sport, where athletes, and often youth athletes, must urinate in front of a doping control officer. While urinating, the athletes must have their pants or shorts pulled down below their knees, and shirts pulled up above their chest. This is done to ensure that no urine samples are tampered with. This practice could be seen as a significant violation of privacy, which is understood as permissible in sport because athletes have diminished privacy rights in the eyes of the law.

The area of doping control that has recently been causing the most controversy among legal scholars pertains to what is termed the "whereabouts rule" (Valkenberg, 2014; Waddington, 2010). The WADA whereabouts rule requires that athletes provide doping control officers with their whereabouts at least 90 days in advance for at least one hour per day during out of season competition. A previous version of the rule was challenged by an Olympic track star, Christine Ohuruogu, after she was suspended for changing her travel plans on three occasions without providing notice and therefore was unavailable for drug testing at the time and location where she was selected for testing. She appealed the suspension to the Court of Arbitration for Sport, which upheld the suspension on the grounds that "out-of-competition testing is at the heart of any effective anti-doping programme" (*Ohuruogu v. UKA & IAAF*, para. 16).

Beyond the constant surveillance that athletes are under throughout the year, their personal information also travels with them to doping control agencies worldwide when they cross borders. Sport does, however, appear to have an exemption around privacy provisions in the interests of protecting competitions from athletes who might use performance-enhancing drugs when they are in the off-season and travelling to far-away destinations outside the reach of doping control officers.

Sport and Human Rights Law

The Human Rights Act (1998) in England makes it unlawful for a public authority to act in a way that is incompatible with the European Convention on Human Rights and Fundamental Freedoms. However, the courts in England have ruled that sports governing bodies are not a "public authority" and therefore sport is exempt from this body of law. It can be argued that sport is a public authority as it is typically funded by public money and the decisions made in sport can have a large public impact; however, the English courts have maintained that it is a private entity. In other jurisdictions, e.g. Canada, sports organizations typically fall under the purview of public law and are susceptible to challenges under human rights legislation.

Exemption from the Human Rights Act in England does not mean, however, that sports organizations are free to discriminate against individuals on protected grounds in the Convention as they like. As an employer, sports organizations must adhere to the Equity Act. They cannot discriminate against their employees, including athletes, or discriminate in their provision of goods and services to the public. For example, in *Sterling v. Leeds Rugby League Cup* (2001), a rugby league player was successful in filing a claim of racial discrimination.

In contrast to racial discrimination, some exemptions on the basis of sex and gender do appear to exist in the governance of sport. Section 195(3) of the Equity Act provides an allowance for sex discrimination in sports of:

> A competitive nature in circumstances in which the physical strength, stamina or physique of average persons of one sex would put them at a disadvantage compared to average persons of the other sex as competitors in events involving the activity.

Likewise, according to Bradford (2005), all anti-discrimination legislation in Australia provides an exception that allows sporting organisations to exclude participants on the basis of their sex where strength, stamina and physique of the athletes are relevant.

In *Bennett v. Football Association and Nottinghamshire Football Association* (unreported decision on July 28, 1998) a ruling that prevented an eleven-year old schoolgirl from playing football with boys was upheld. In *Taylor v. Moorabbin Saints* the courts ruled that a thirteen-year old girl could not be excluded from competing against boys of her age in Australian Rules Football, but that fourteen- and fifteen-year old girls could be excluded. The arguments presented were that girls will be at high risk to get hurt competing against boys who are physically stronger, and that the inclusion of girls in boy's sport would lessen the competitive nature of the sport. Via these outdated, stereotypical notions of sex and gender an exception for sport and discrimination has been established.

Exceptions from Freedom of Religion rights also appear to exist in the context of sport. The Amateur Boxing Association of England (ABAE) requires that all boxers be clean-shaven for safety reasons (Cottrell, 2010). Boxing officials have made the case that facial hair has the risk of scratching the eye of opponents when competitors become tied up, that beards rubbing on an opponent's face can further open up gashes, and that it is difficult for medical staff to locate and treat open wounds within facial hair. In some religious faiths, beards hold significant meaning, e.g. Sikhism. Requiring boxers to be clean-shaven could be considered a violation on Freedom of Religion. The ABAE contends, however, that their rule is proportionate and justified and at present sport appears to be exempted on these grounds for such rules.

Sport and Labour/Employment Law

Although organized sport is often a workplace for many people including athletes, labour and employment laws do not often appear to apply to sport workplaces. To provide one example, professional athletes in most states in the United States are not able to file for workplace compensation for injuries that they sustained while playing their sports. In fact, the State of California recently enacted a workplace compensation exemption for sport into law in Bill AB 1309, which prohibits athletes who spent most of their careers playing for teams outside California from filing compensation claims in the state (Emamdjomeh & Bensinger, 2014). In what other workplace in

North America can a worker be severely injured in the course of their work, fired because of their injury, and then denied compensation for the injury?

To provide another example, it is standard for workplace health and safety acts, across different jurisdictions, to have provisions that make violence and harassment in the workplace unlawful. In the workplaces of professional boxing, hockey, football, and rugby, committing acts of extreme physical aggression and verbally taunting opponents are part of the everyday work. In fact, declining to engage in such violent acts, e.g. a boxer who refuses to throw any punches, would lead to a shortened career in the profession. To preserve the traditions of sports, which often involve elements of violence that would be completely unacceptable and unlawful in any other workplace, sport appears to have some exemptions from workplace health and safety laws.

Sport and Criminal Law

One area of law where public criticism is often waged against judiciaries for their failure to uphold laws is in relation to violence in sport, and assault laws in particular. For example, in the violent sport of Canadian gridiron football, there has not been a single case where a professional athlete has been criminally charged for violence on the field (Fogel, 2013). This is a sport where catastrophic injuries are commonplace, yet the courts have allowed Canadian football to self-govern violence.

In contrast, however, Canadian ice hockey has not been afforded the same exception. In a select few cases, Canadian hockey players have appeared in Canadian courts. Of those, even fewer have resulted in successful convictions by the prosecution. A primary reason for this is the legal notion of *volenti non fit injuria*, or "to a willing person, injury is not done" (Corbett, Findlay, & Lech, 2008, p. 28). That is, there is a basic understanding that if an act of violence in sport is consented to, that no crime has occurred.

The consent defence does not, however, give sport an absolute exception from assault law. In *R. v. McSorley* (2000), Canadian professional hockey player Marty McSorley violently struck his stick against the head of an opposing player Donald Brashear, who he had engaged in consensual fighting with earlier in the game, and was charged with assault with a deadly weapon. Four years later, another professional hockey player, Todd Bertuzzi, appeared in Canadian courts for an incidence of violence in professional ice hockey. In this incident, Todd Bertuzzi struck another player, Steve Moore, in the back of the head with his gloved fist, resulting in two broken vertebra and brain injuries that subsequently ended his hockey career. Bertuzzi was given a conditional discharge on the grounds that he serve 80 hours of community service.

Non-players can also be held liable for injuries in sport. For example, in *Smolden v. Whitworth* (1997) and *Vowles v. Evans* (2003) the referees of two separate rugby matches were both held liable for the injuries that players sustained as a result of undue care by the referees in keeping control over the game. In a Canadian case, a high school football player sought damages from a Board of Education because of a broken neck he sustained during play that he argued was a result of improper coaching (*Thomas [Next friend of] v. Hamilton Board of Education, 1994*). Similarly, in *Dunn v. University of Ottawa* (1995), a Canadian university football player successfully sought damages from the coach of the opposing team for failing to adequately control his players and coaching staff, which ultimately led to his injury.

In England, an important legal precedent for sports violence was established in 1981, though it was not in the context of sport (*A-G's Reference*, 1981). In this particular case, two young men aged engaged in a fistfight that led to injuries. Though it was consented to, the fighting was deemed to not be in the public interest. As such, the boys were not given a legal exemption from assault law. However, it is through this provision that violence in sport can continue without interference from the courts providing it can be shown to be in the public interest. As such, a public interest exception appears to exist in relation to sports violence in England, which allows for the continuation of violent sports like mixed-martial arts, rugby, and boxing.

Sport and EU Law

The area of law that appears to clash with sports governance most frequently in European countries in recent years is the broad area of EU law. Where EU law clashes with sport governance is typically in the establishment of sport rules that have the potential to provide unfair financial advantage, restrict freedom of movement of people, or restrict freedom to provide services.

For the 1998 World Cup football tournament hosted in and won by France, approximately 750,000 tickets were reserved for people who had a postal code in France. Locals bought the tickets and then sold them at inflated prices to foreign visitors, giving citizens of France a competitive economic advantage. French football officials argued that the sale to local residents was done as a precaution to limit conflict and violence during matches. The courts ruled that there was no reasonable sport-specific justification for the postal code rule, and that since it had clear economic implications it was in violation of EU law (*Decision*, 2000). The courts ensured that a rule of a governing body of sport could not be used to financial benefit the citizens of one nation over others, without a valid sport-related justification.

Many cases have come before the courts on the question of sports rules restricting the freedom of movement of people/workers, e.g. *Bosman*,[4] *Walgrave and Koch*,[5] *Dona*,[6] *Deliège*,[7] *Lehtonen*,[8] *Kolpak*,[9] and *Simutenkov*.[10] The result of these cases has

---

[4] Footballer, Jean-Marc Bosman, faced financial restrictions on transferring between clubs in different countries of the European Union, seeking to move from Belgium to France. He sued for restraint of trade under EU law.
[5] Bruno Walgrave and Norbert Koch were pacemakers for cycling events. They challenged a rule that required pacemakers to be of a particular nationality.
[6] Footballer, Gaetano Dona, brought forward a challenge against rules that limited the right to take part in certain football matches to citizens of a particular country.
[7] Christelle Deliège, a Belgian judoka, challenged rules that limited the number of Judo competitors from each country that could compete in international Judo competitions.
[8] Finish basketball player, Jyri Lehtonen, challenged the legality of transfer window rules, which limited him from being able to switch from a Finish to Belgian team because he did not do so during the specified transfer period.
[9] Slovak handball player, Maros Kolpak, challenged a rule in a German league that placed limits on the number of non-EU players a team could have on its roster.

been to establish that governing bodies of sport cannot create rules that prohibit the free movement of athletes across national borders, with exceptions granted only if there is a justified sporting reason such as establishing competitions between nations like the Olympics or FIFA World Cup.

Some athletes have also argued that anti-doping policies violate their right to freedom of providing services, as positive tests are typically accompanied by mandatory suspensions that restrict athletes from participating in their livelihood. In *Edwards* (1998),[11] the presiding judge ruled that prohibiting athletes from taking banned substances was a rule of a purely sporting nature with no economic purpose. Likewise, in *Meca-Medina* (2006),[12] anti-doping rules were again upheld on the basis that they served no definitive economic purpose and were central to the governing rules of the sport. Furthermore, anti-doping regulations were perceived by the courts to fulfill important function of competitive balance in sport and safeguarding the health of athletes.

Conclusion

Some very specific sporting exceptions do and should exist. Sport has certain unique properties that justify some exceptions from law, such as the need to maintain competitive balance between teams, to ensure safety of participants, to retain some autonomy from political and government influence, and to maintain the integrity of the game. Specificity of sport allows for legal exceptions providing there are no unfair economic implications of sporting rules and governance, that rules are purely in the interest of sport, and that any sporting exemptions are made in public interest.

No state of exception from sport exists in the form that Agamben describes. By the very fact that clashes between legislation, law, and sport continue to occur, it can be seen that no pure state of exception from the laws of the land exist. Legal exceptions, are, however, made on a case-by-case basis at the ongoing and ever-changing discretion of the courts. The sporting exceptions that do exist are not absolute or unconditional. The courts have, to date, been very careful to not give governing bodies in sport an open exception from treaties, laws, and legislation. While the courts do grant governing bodies of sport many freedoms to govern themselves alongside certain specific exceptions, these freedoms are not without constraint of the law and judicial oversight. The law is intended to be flexible and reasonable; modest sporting exceptions are a reflection of this basic nature of law.

---

[10] Russian footballer, Igor Simutenkov, challenged a rule in a Spanish league that limited the number of non-Spanish players who could play in a national competition.

[11] An amateur athlete, Edwards, challenged the legality of a refusal of the British Athletics Federation to reinstate him after an appeal of his suspension of four years after testing positive for the use of banned anabolic steroids.

[12] Two swimmers, David Meca-Medina and Igor Majcen, were banned for four years following positive tests for a prohibited substance. The two swimmers aimed to prove that anti-doping rules were in breach of EU competition law as it restricted their economic freedom to pursue their careers.

Chapter 3

Policing Femininity: Intersex Discrimination in International Athletics

Introduction

The fourth fundamental principle of the Olympic Charter states: "The practice of sport is a human right. Every individual must have the possibility of practicing sport, without discrimination of any kind" (IOC, 2013, p. 11). Despite this principle, the historical practices of the International Olympic Committee (IOC) and International Association of Athletics (IAAF) have been that every individual who fits neatly into the sex binary of male or female must have the possibility of practicing sport without discrimination of any kind. Athletes whose biologies do not fit neatly into the sex binary have faced a long history of exclusion from participation in the Olympics and international athletics competitions. This has been done largely on the grounds of outdated sex stereotyping based on assumptions about the physical superiority of men (Pieper, 2016). Through the decades, female athletes have had to undergo a number of different tests from "nude parades," to chromosome assessment, to DNA analysis, which are aimed at policing their femininity and ensuring that no competitive advantage is permitted in women's sport on the basis of sex attributes (Adair, 2011). This has been a highly controversial practice, particularly since male athletes do not go through similar tests. However, some argue that sex verification testing is a necessity to ensure integrity and competitive balance in women's athletics (see Turner, 2016).

This chapter opens with a discussion of the sex binary in medicine, law, and sport, and defines relevant terms and identifies the processes by which individuals are categorized as male or female. The history of controversial sex testing in athletics, which has added further impetus to the policing of femininity in sport, is then overviewed. The discussion then moves to examining the legal aspects of sex testing and the exclusion of intersex individuals from participation. This chapter concludes by highlighting a range of possible resolutions to the controversy, and makes an argument that it is possible to strike a balanced position of maintaining fundamental human rights and ensuring the continued integrity and competitive balance in international athletics.

The Sex Binary in Medicine, Law, and Sport

With few exceptions internationally, when a baby is born a doctor is faced with a choice: male or female. Some countries, such as Australia, now recognize a third category of sex: non-specified. In the vast majority of births, the male or female distinction is based on a visual assessment of the newborn's genital organs and an assessment of whether a functional penis is present or not. The government records the doctor's decision on the child's Birth Certificate, as well as subsequent documents throughout the life course, e.g. passports, driver's licences, etc.

In medicine and in law, a sex binary exists where individuals are categorized as either male or female. The term sex refers specifically to the biological characteristics of male and female that are determined by factors such as genitals, gonads, chromosomes, and hormones. It is common to see the terms sex and gender used interchangeably, however, there are important distinctions in how they are defined. While sex is rooted in biological characteristics, gender refers to the socio-cultural characteristics that are typically associated with a particular sex, e.g. styles of dress, hair length, colour preferences, etc. (Oakley, 2015). The two terms are intricately linked, but distinct in definition, as well as in law.

Not all newborns fit neatly into the categories of male and female. One medical estimate is that 1.7 percent of all live births do not conform to this binary but, rather, fall somewhere in between (Blackless et al., 2000). These newborns are classified as intersexed; that is, they possess characteristics of both male and female in terms of chromosomes (X and Y), gonads (testes or ovaries), genitals (penis/scrotum or clitoris/labia), phenotypes (secondary sex characteristics like body hair and breast tissue), hormones (androgens or estrogens), and so forth (Greenberg, 1999). The notion of sex as a binary of male and female is a social construct (Laquer, 1990). While various characteristics that determine sex are biological, these characteristics are often not congruent with a designation of male or female. The result in most countries is that individuals get placed in the category of male or female, often with a diagnosis of a sexual development disorder.

The Intersex Society of North America lists 18 different disorders of sexual development (DSDs) that can stem from genetics, hormones, and/or ambiguity in genitals including: 1) 5-alpha reductase deficiency, 2) androgen insensitivity syndrome (AIS), 3) aphalia, 4) clitoromegaly (large clitoris), 5) congenital adrenal hyperplasia (CAH), 6) gonadal dysgenisis, 7) hypospadias, 8) klinefelter syndrome, 9) micropenis, 10) mosaicism involving sex hormones, 11) MRKH (congenital absence of vagina), 12) ovo-testes (formerly known as hermaphroditism), 13) partial androgen insensitivity syndrome (PAIS), 14) progestin induced viralization, 15) swyer syndrome, and 16) turner syndrome (ISNA, n.d.). Seen by the medical establishment as conditions, doctors seek to provide treatment, typically in the form of surgeries and or hormone therapy. The aim is to treat intersex individual so that they can be placed in the medical and legal categories of male and female.

The term intersex is sometimes used interchangeably with transsexual and transgender, but these terms all have different meanings. Unlike intersex, which refers to individuals who are born with both male and female sex characteristics, transsexual refers to individuals who have a strong desire to assume the physical characteristics and gender presentation of the opposite sex to which they have been assigned at birth. Some individuals seek surgery and hormone therapy to attain congruence (Greenberg, 2012). Transgender is typically conceived of as a broader term, similar to queer, that refers to an identity some people adopt when their assigned sex (determined by the doctor), gender identity (how they see themselves), and gender presentations (how they dress and present themselves to the outside world) are not aligned. Individuals whose sex assignment, gender identity, and gender presentation align are referred to as cisgender (Greenberg, 2012).

Most social institutions make an assumption that the populations they serve are all cisgender. This is exemplified in institutional forms that force individual to identify themselves as either male or female. Likewise, most public buildings have two washrooms: one for men and one for women. Although, in recent years, with the increasing recognition of transgender rights, this has begun to change with the introduction of gender-neutral washrooms.

History of Sex Testing in Athletics

The social institution of sport lags even further behind in recognizing sex and gender beyond a rigid socially constructed dichotomy (Pieper, 2016). In sport, individuals are classified as male or female and are often forced to participate on either male or female sports teams. For those individuals whose sex and gendered identities sit outside the cisgender dichotomy, this practice can create significant barriers to their participation in sport. The institution of sport is unique from most other social institutions, however, in that medical and legal determinations of sex have traditionally not been seen as valid classification mechanisms of who is to be considered male and who is to be considered female. Instead, major institutions of sport, such as the IOC and IAAF, have sought to devise their own mechanisms for determining sex and separating athletes into those who qualify to compete and those who do not.

In elite athletics, there has been a long-held concern, based on out-of-date stereotypes of biologically-based male athletic superiority, that a) some men will try to cheat and will pose as women to win in sport, which can be termed "sex fraud" (Reeser, 2005), and b) that some women will possess male sex characteristics that will give them an unfair advantage over their competition. This has given rise to a long history of ever-changing methods for determining sex, which can at best be described as policing femininity. This term usefully highlights the point that sex testing in sport is not based on a concern of women posing as men to compete in male sports. Instead, it is based on a concern of whether or not a female athlete has the appropriate feminine characteristics to compete against other women.

Until 1928, women were largely excluded from participation in international athletics competitions, including the Olympic Games (Smith, 1998). When women's sports were introduced to the Olympics, there was a concern that men might try to masquerade as women to stand a greater likelihood of winning events. Despite this concern, sex testing by the IOC and IAAF has never uncovered a case of a male athlete knowingly disguising his sex to compete in women's sport (Ritchie et al., 2008). This concern has been a moral panic, of sorts, without a real basis in reality.

The early years of women's participation in Olympic and international athletics competitions were marred with controversy sparked by accusations that certain women not possessing appropriately feminine bodily characteristics were men masquerading as women (Pieper, 2016). For example, in the 1936 Berlin Olympics, two female sprinters, Stella Walsh and Helen Stephens, were suspected of being men. Walsh was dubbed in the media "Stella the Fella." In the same Olympics, a German high jumper, Dora Ratjen, was accused of bounding her alleged male genitals in order to participate in the women's competition, in which she placed fourth. These cases and others remain controversial as to the sex of the athletes, though their birth documents indicate that they were women. In the case of Stella Walsh, later postmortem tests in 1980 revealed that she had "ambiguous genitalia" (Peterson, 2010).

Since then, others have continued to argue that Ratjen was, in fact, a man and was supported by a corrupt Nazi regime trying to increase the German medal count (Glazer, 2012). A large-scale investigation revealed that Ratjen was born female, but had male characteristics and later came to identify as a man, though medical tests have shown that he did not have a penis capable of reproduction (Large, 2007). What now appears most likely is that these and many other athletes who had their femininity questioned in the early Olympics were intersex athletes who had been medically and legally defined as women and identified as women.

Continued controversies over appropriate feminine body characteristics in elite women's athletics, and Cold War political concerns of the Soviet Union using men posing as women to increase their medal counts, prompted the IAAF to create a policy requiring female athletes to "pass a femininity test." The tests were referred to as "nude parades" and required all female athletes to undergo a visual examination of their naked bodies and genitals to determine if they were feminine enough to compete with other women (Adair, 2011). Women who were appropriately feminine were given a "Certificate of Femininity" and were cleared for competition (Rupert, 2011).

Because the visual tests were eventually deemed to be degrading and humiliating for female athletes, and coinciding the establishment of the IOC Medical Commission, visual tests were replaced with genetic testing in 1968 (Rupert, 2011). The sex chromatin test, sometimes termed the "Barr Body Test," involved a microscopic examination of cells obtained from a buccal swab to look for the presence of the barr body and/or absence of the Y chromosome (Rupert, 2011). Across the Winter Olympics in Grenoble and the Summer Olympics in Mexico City, only one female athlete, Ewa Klobukowska, failed the test (Gandert et al., 2013). Klobukowska was permanently disqualified from future events, stripped of her records, and was forced to return her Olympic medals from the 1960 Olympics. She was deemed male for the purposes of sport, although records indicate that she later gave birth to a child and that medically and legally she was considered female.

The barr test continued to be used until 1992. Between 1968 and 1992 it is estimated that, on average, less that one female athlete failed the test per year from the Olympics and international athletics competitions (Gandert et al., 2013). In cases of failed tests, most women withdrew from the competitions. In fact, reports indicate that they were encouraged to fake injuries to justify withdrawing from competitions and retiring from their sport early. In one case, however, a Spanish hurler, Maria Jose Martinez-Patino, challenged the ruling that she failed a femininity test and fought to continue competing. It was discovered that she had a XY karyotype and androgen insensitivity. Despite having female physical characteristics (breasts and a vagina), she was banned from athletics. She successfully argued that her condition did not give her an athletic advantage and she was reinstated three years after her first failed test. However, she faced public humiliation and failed to qualify for the 1992 Summer Olympics (Gandert et al., 2013).

It has been speculated that the Martinez-Patino case led the IOC to question the effectiveness and appropriateness of the barr test (Reeser, 2005). Combined with the discovery of DNA and its applications in the 1980s, the IOC developed a new sex verification test for the 1992 Winter Olympics in Albertville. The new test involved "a polymerase chain reaction (PCR) determination of the absence or presence of DNA sequences from the testes-determining gene located on the Y chromosome" (Reeser, 2005, p. 553).

Drawing on criticisms of various physicians, geneticists, ethicists, and feminists, it was resolved at the 1996 World Conference on Women and Health that sex testing should be abolished. The IOC Athletes Commission later supported this resolution in 1999 (Rupert, 2011). The thrusts of the sex testing abolition arguments were that: a) tests were faulty, b) the tests measured characteristics of sex that did not physical advantages in competition, c) the tests were discriminatory as only women were tested, and d) the necessary supports were not in place to help women deal with the physiological, and psychological aspects of a failed test. The Canadian Academy of Sports Medicine put forward the recommendation that "individuals who were raised as female and [were] psychologically and socially female from childhood should be eligible to compete in women's competition regardless of their chromosomal, gonadal and hormonal sex" (Doig, 1997).

In 1999, the IOC conditionally removed the requirement that female athletes undergo sex verification, with the caveat that testing could still be done on a case-by-case basis if there was reasonable cause for suspicion of an athlete's sex (Allen, 2016). Over the past fifteen years, the IOC and IAAF have further formalized case-by-case policies, whereby women—and only women—are sex tested when there is a concern that they lack femininity. This testing is now done by a panel of experts, which includes psychiatrists, urologists, endocrinologists, and geneticists. Athletes who test positive for undefined overly masculine characteristics can typically continue competing after undergoing surgery and/or hormone therapy to construct what the expert panel deems appropriate femininity.

The most publicized case in recent years of a female athlete being investigated for lacking feminine physical qualities is that of South African athlete Caster Semenya. At the Track and Field World Championships in 2009 in Berlin, Semenya torched the 800-meter competition by 2.45 seconds. Her competitors openly doubted that she was a woman given her speed and large, well-defined muscles. Amidst these suspicions, the IAAF asked Semenya to undergo sex testing. The IAAF did not release a formal statement on the findings, but the findings were leaked in the press that although Semenya had the external genitalia of a woman, she had internal testes, which disqualified her from further female competition (Hurst, 2009). Alleging that sex testing in sport is both sexist and racist, the South African government filed a complaint to the UN on behalf of Semenya (Swarr et al., 2009). It is not officially known what surgical or hormonal treatment conditions she had to undergo, but

Semenya has been since reinstated and won a silver medal in the 2012 Summer Olympics in London, and gold medal in the 2016 Summer Olympics in Rio de Janeiro.

Leading up the qualifiers for the 2016 Summer Olympics, the IOC and IAAF have continued with the case-by-case model of sex testing rather than compulsory testing for all women. However, the burden of suspicion was heightened and does not allow for testing brought about by accusations of rival competitors. Reasonable grounds for testing have included: a) an athlete requesting that she be tested, b) preliminary results from a routine medical examination or physical, c) results from a doping control test, or d) the receipt of confidential information from an IAAF official (IAAF, 2011). There is also an acknowledgement that not all intersex characteristics even have the potential for heightened athletic performance; the focus is now predominantly on elevated testosterone and hyperandrogenism (IOC, 2012).

POTENTIAL INTERSEX DISCRIMINATION LEGAL CHALLENGES

Internationally, few legal systems provide any protected status to intersex persons. As such, the term intersex discrimination is somewhat of a misnomer in a legal sense. Sex testing could more accurately be seen in law as a form of sex discrimination, in that it is differential treatment on the basis of sex, as male athletes are not tested for sex development disorders. It is only women who undergo such tests and face the loss of their livelihoods. Furthermore, intersex persons who are tested in sport have already been medically and legally defined as female at birth, and likely identify as women if they are competing as women in sport. Governing bodies of sport, such as the IOC and IAAF, have taken it upon themselves to deny the right of some women to identify as a woman and be free to participate in sport as such. Intersex discrimination is, therefore, a form of sex discrimination.

Glazer (2012) suggests that the best legal recourse for a woman who has been disqualified on the basis of sex testing results would be to bring forward a civil lawsuit in the country in which the athletics event she has been disqualified from is being staged (Glazer, 2012). This could be possible, but such an approach raises an issue of jurisdiction. For example, in *Sagen v. Vancouver Committee for the 2010 Olympic and Paralympic Games (VANOC)*, a group of female ski jumpers brought forward a claim of discrimination against the Vancouver-based organizing committee of the 2010 Winter Olympics. The claim made by the skiers was that not including a women's ski jumping event was discriminatory under the Canadian Charter and Rights and Freedoms, under section 15 on equity rights. While the Canadian court found that the Charter does apply to VANOC, and that not including women's ski jumping was discriminatory, it was determined that it was IOC policy that was discriminatory and not the actions of VANOC. The Canadian court could do nothing to repeal a policy or practice of the IOC. While this was not a case of intersex discrimination, it does indicate the difficulties of using local courts to take on an international governing body in sport.

Cooper (2010) argues that the most viable legal recourse for intersex athletes is through human rights complaints. For instance, the Universal Declaration of Human

Rights (UDHR) states, "everyone has the right to freely participate in the cultural life of the community" (UN, 1948). Access to sports participation is a fundamental right, for which the IOC agrees in their Olympic Charter. The Brighton Declaration on Women and Sport (2012), brought forward by the British Sports Council, states the aim of ensuring "that all women and girls have opportunity to participate in sport in a safe and supportive environment which preserves the rights, dignity, and respect of individuals" (p. 1). Sex testing violates this provision in multiple ways, as it can exclude women from sport and does not preserve the dignity of individuals where women are paraded as men in the media for having a sex development disorder.

The Beijing Declaration and Platform for Action, which the IAAF and IOC have agreed to, aims to "support the advancement of women in all areas of athletics and physical activity" (Beijing Declaration, 1995, Section 83.k). Again, sex testing and the exclusionary practices that can follow is a form of sex discrimination, violating the rights of women to participate. While it can be shown that sex testing violates fundamental human rights, these declarations are not binding in law. As declarations, they are statements of moral commitments to encourage nations and organizations that are signatories to enact laws and policies that do not violate the provisions. Despite this, appeals to the United Nations, such as the one brought forward by the South African government in the Caster Semenya sex verification tests and mishandling, should be encouraged to place pressure on organizations to repeal femininity policing policies and practices in sport.

Furthermore, there are legally binding human rights laws that could be appealed to in challenging sex verification test results, and the overall practice in general. For example, the Convention on the Elimination of All Forms of Discrimination Against Women (CEDAW) became an international treaty in 1981. Various Articles are of relevance; particularly, Article 13 specifically identifies that women should have "the same opportunities to participate actively in sports and physical education" (UN, 1979, Article 10.g). As of January 1, 2008 the responsibility for hearing complaints has been transferred from the UN to the Office of the High Commissioner for Human Rights in Geneva. This could provide a stage of repealing femininity repealing in sport.

Beyond the straightforward human rights violations of excluding medically and legally defined women from sport and compromising their privacy and dignity in the process, the Coalition for the Inclusion of Athletes in Sport have argued that the IOC's current guidelines for suspicion-based sex testing violate international human rights law, and the IOC's own commitments to equality, inclusion, and fair play, in the following ways: 1) by pathologizing gender ambiguities that are part of a normal spectrum of human variation, 2) by assuming that masculine traits give advantages to female athletes, but that feminine traits give no advantage to male athletes, 3) by not stating clear criteria for the determination of male and female, which is excessively discretionary and subjective, and 4) by subjecting only certain women to the policy through witch hunts and requesting they undergo body modification to ensure appropriate femininity (Coalition, 2016). It seems highly unlikely that a human rights tribunal would simply overlook these glaring problems with sex verification testing just to preserve a false notion of competitive balance in sport. This is a human rights issue, and therefore a viable response is to pursue human rights complaints through declarations and conventions that protect the rights of women internationally.

Another approach to appealing the results of a sex verification test is to bring forward an appeal to CAS. The fundamental purpose of establishing CAS was to have a legal institution that could provide jurisdiction for international sports-related disputes. This need grew largely out of a high-demand from appeals related to violations of the WADA Code, but CAS has a larger purpose to remedy disputes in sport beyond doping. In fact, the IOC Regulations on Female Hyperandrogenism state that the court of appeal for IOC decisions is CAS, which go so far as to specify that "the time to file an appeal to CAS shall be within twenty-one (21) days from the date of communication by the IOC to the appealing party of the decision" (IOC, 2012).

In 2014, the suitability of an appeal to overturn a suspension following a sex verification test was confirmed. A female sprinter from India, Dutee Chand, was suspended from competition after testing positive for a male biological characteristic. Specifically, her testosterone levels were perceived as too high for a woman. She successfully appealed the suspension in a CAS hearing (*Chand v. Athletics Federation of India (AFI) and IAAF*, 2014). It was ruled that a clear link had not been established between heightened testosterone and a direct advantage in athletics. CAS has given the IAAF a two-year window to bring forward direct scientific evidence that establishes a causal link. While the IAAF has vowed that they will do so, they had not by the time of the 2016 Summer Olympics, which allowed Dutee Chand and other athletes with potential intersex characteristics to compete without sex verification testing. If the IAAF fail to prove a direct scientific link, the decision will be final.

Possible Resolutions for Fairness in Athletics

For the reasons stated above, sex testing policies and procedures in sport would likely not be upheld in a human rights tribunal or CAS. While the case law on sex-verification testing in international athletics is modest, it is clear that the historical and current practices are excessive, discriminatory, and unfair. The question then becomes, how should intersex athletes be included in international athletics? And, how can this be done in a way that balances fundamental human rights and fairness in sport?

One possibility is to have women who have tested positive for male characteristics to compete in male competitions. This would not be all that different from the National Collegiate Athletics Association's (NCAA) approach to transitioned athletes. The NCAA policy requires that men who transition to women continue to compete with men, while women who transition to men must compete with men (Zigler & Huntley, 2013). While this might assuage the feelings of those who continue to believe in the myth of a fair playing field in sport and stereotypes of masculine athletic superiority, it would remain discriminatory, would restrict access to sport for some women, and would create an unfair spectacular for female athletes who want to compete as women against women. This is not a viable option.

Another possibility could be to create a third segregated division in sport for intersex athletes. This is highly impractical because the number of intersex athletes is not likely to be high enough to allow for suitable competitions. While no definitive numbers are publically available that show exactly how many female athletes have failed sex verification tests over the past 50 years, it can be estimated that it is less than 50. Of those, only a few have characteristics that could possibly be seen as having a competitive advantage. This would also cause an unfair spectacle for female intersex athletes who want to compete as women, limiting their opportunities for sport participation. It could also have devastating consequences, e.g. it has been reported that runner Santhi Soundarajan, who won the silver medal in the 2006 Asian Games, attempted suicide in 2007 after tests showed that she was not female and she was stripped of her records and medals and subjected to intense public scrutiny (Gandert et al., 2013). In this climate, a segregated intersex division is not a viable option.

A third option would be to remove sex segregation in athletics entirely, and instead create a complex classification system to come closer to truly leveling the playing field. The beginnings of this model already exist in Paralympic sport. Athletes who compete in the Paralympics are grouped into ten major categories based on the type of disability they have, e.g. visually impaired runners compete against other visually impaired runners (Britain, 2009). This type of classification is also somewhat present in certain existing events with weight classes, e.g. wrestling and boxing. Hypothetically, this model could be expanded to all international athletics events and competitions. This model is not, however, would require a monumental change to the way in which athletics are organized throughout the world. To ensure actual even playing fields would also require a highly complex classification system, e.g. a weighted score that factors in height, weight, playing experience, socioeconomic background, climate and altitude of training country, etc. Furthermore, due to sociocultural factors that have held many women back from advancing as far as men with athletic achievements, this type of classification system would likely be exclusionary to female athletes in the short-term. While a move away from sex segregation in sport towards a different means of classification might be possible at some point in human history, this is not a viable option at this moment or in the near future.

A clearly viable option could simply be to abolish sex verification testing altogether and allow women to compete as women. Sex verification testing has been done because of concerns over sex fraud and competitive imbalance. Both of these rationales are illogical starting points that do not justify excluding women from sport and publicly humiliating them in the process. The original notion of men dressing up as women to compete in women's sport that led to sex verification testing remains an absurd one. This is especially the case in an era of intense media scrutiny around sport, and the broadcasting of private lives in public spaces via social media. Committing gender fraud in sport would require a well-orchestrated plan from the point of birth, and highly complex organizing throughout one's involvement in sport; such an athlete would need to avoid the shower room and convincingly wear a form-fitted spandex suit used for most track-and-field events. Furthermore, as Rupert points out, "at any given time, there are only a handful of men in the world who could beat the best women, and most of them would be so well known in the sport that their disappearance would be noted, as would the sudden appearance in the top ranks of a previously unknown female competitor" (2011, p. 346). Furthermore, WADA doping control officers watch athletes closely when they urinate to ensure they are not cheating the doping test; it would be difficult for a man to hide his penis while urinating and pass himself off as a female athlete.

There is no basis for testing on the grounds of sex fraud. Even if a child's parents had the corrupt idea to raise a boy as a girl so that he might someday pass-off as a female athlete, the chances are he would not be at the level to compete against the world's best female athletes. While there are some sociocultural and biological differences that have led to variation in sporting performance between men and women, these differences are not so vast that any man will be a superior athlete to a woman. The fastest women in the world run the 100m in less than a second less than the fastest men, with an ever-shrinking time gap from year-to-year (Holden, 2004). The hypothetical boy passing off as a girl would most likely be an inferior athlete and would have no competitive advantages. Men are not going to pretend to be women to participate in women's sport. And, even if they could pull off such an extraordinary fraud, the likelihood that they would even be competitive in women's sport is miniscule.

A basic premise of sport is that competitors are not equal. They are of different height, weight, muscle-fibre composition, sociocultural backgrounds, etc. There is thus no such thing as an even playing field. Yao Ming is 7'6, which gave him a huge competitive advantage in the sport of basketball. The IOC did not exclude him from representing China in the Olympics because he was at the far end of the height spectrum of natural human variation, which gave him a competitive advantage in his sport. Likewise, as Cooper (2010) has outlined, Michael Phelps—who has won fourteen Olympic gold medals in swimming—is widely celebrated for his athletic accomplishments that are rooted largely in natural advantages. Phelps has very particular physiological advantages over his competition such as an abnormally long torso, broad shoulders, an arm-span that significantly exceeds his height, size 14 feet, and very flexible ankles that can flex fifteen degrees past what is considered normal (Cooper, 2010). Physically, he is considered abnormal and through training he has learned to utilized these abnormalities and become an Olympic champion.

If Phelps can be permitted to compete and win fourteen gold medals, then why are women who have anatomy that does not conform to what is deemed to be "normal" not free to compete in sport without sex testing or required medical treatments? Targeting a specific population of athletes (women) and isolating a specific, a naturally occurring variation between them (masculine characteristics) to establish grounds of exclusion is blatantly discriminatory. Sex verification testing is inequitable, unethical, unfair, and illogical. It should be abolished.

Conclusion

A woman who is recognized in law as a woman should be eligible to compete in women's athletics competitions. Denying women access to sport, or requiring that they undergo body modification, to continue to compete on the basis of naturally occurring variations is discriminatory. It is also illogical, based on a false notion of competitive balance and an even playing field in sport. The playing field is not even in sport, it has never been even, and it never will be even. While placing limits on the use of performance-enhancing substances can be seen as a reasonable restriction on athletes, doing so is by-and-large a health and safety concern. Intersex characteristics are naturally occurring forms of human variation much like height, flexibility, arm-length, and muscle-fibre composition. Limits are not placed on these naturally occurring variations; in fact, elite sport is somewhat of a celebration of individuals with unique genetics and physical advantages.

Sex verification testing is particularly problematic in that it is directed purely towards female athletes. Male athletes have not been tested, nor are there any indications that they will be in the future. It is seemingly acceptable for male athletes to have naturally occurring genetic variations that give them advantages in their sport and allow them to set athletic world records. In contrast, IOC and IAAF policies and practices have ensured that there are limits placed on the acceptability of variation of female athletes. As the gender gap in athletic performance continues to shrink, to the point where experts are now beginning to predict that female athletes will eventually surpass men in running times of various events, it can been seen that sex verification testing is a deliberate act to hold the progress of female athletes back (Pieper, 2016). Caster Semenya was eighteen-years old when she won the 800m race in the Track and Field World Championships in 2009. Though she was the gold medalist at the 2016 Summer Olympics in Rio de Janeiro, she would not have won the men's event with her time. Had the IAAF not intervened in her training several years ago, delayed her career, and required undisclosed surgical and/or hormonal treatments, where would she be today? The IAAF and IOC did not give us the opportunity to know the answer to that question.

CHAPTER 4

Breaking Uneven: Legal and Competitive Issues of UEFA's Financial Fair Play Regulations

INTRODUCTION

In recent years, spending on player salaries has increased significantly in UEFA (the Union of European Football Associations) (Hytner, 2013). The spending of well-established, affluent football clubs has placed pressure on other clubs to spend inordinate amounts to attract top-level talent and remain competitive (Davies, 2012), which Ryan Knight (2013) refers to as the "snowball effect" (p. 116). Spending on player salaries remains the largest impediment to the profitability of football clubs (Nicoliello and Zampatti, 2016). Despite heightened revenues, over-spending on players has driven some clubs to the point of potential bankruptcy. According to UEFA, the total deficit of European football clubs in 2012 was €2.036 billion, which increased from €453 million in 2009 (Muller, Lammert, and Hovemann, 2012). UEFA's solution to these financial issues has been the development of Financial Fair Play (FFP) regulations to "introduce more discipline and rationality in club football finances" (UEFA, 2011, p. 1), preventing clubs from becoming financial unfeasible. Underlying the regulations is a sentiment that clubs are not able to self-regulate spending and that clubs must break-even to remain financially stable and thus, UEFA has a responsibility to regulate club spending to ensure the long-term sustainability of European football. Unlike salary cap regulations used in many professional North America leagues that restrict sport teams to minimum and maximum expenditures, the FFP regulations do not stipulate fixed amounts that can be spent on player salaries. Instead, UEFA clubs that make more money can spend more, while teams that make less money must spend less (Schubert, 2014). FFP regulations center on protecting teams from overspending to ensure they break even and do not go into financial insolvency, which would disrupt the stability of UEFA.

Determination of whether or not a club has abided by FFP regulations is largely based on a mathematical formula, whereby total expenditures cannot significantly exceed total revenue. This is the break-even rule that is at the core of the regulations. Clubs must report their financials for this determination to be made. Club spending on transfers, player salaries, and employee salaries are counted as expenditures, while income from ticket sales, broadcasting, merchandising, selling players, and prize money is considered revenue (Long, 2012). Money spent on infrastructure, training facilities, and/or youth development is not included in the assessment. There are some cost exclusions that still allow football clubs to run at a deficit in certain circumstances, such as sales or depreciation of fixed assets like a stadium, career ending injury costs, or losses sustained by the withdrawal of a major club sponsor.

Clubs that are found to have exceeded their allowable spending face UEFA sanctions including fines, transfer embargos, exclusion from competition, and licence withdrawal (Long, 2012).

The solution posed by UEFA to curb financial hardships of its member clubs is to impose costly fines, enact limits on employing better talent, and restrict access to playing on a larger stage with better profits to be made. Schubert (2014) suggests that FFP regulations put football clubs in complicated conflict of interests whereby their performance objectives of meeting FFP regulations, fielding competitive teams that spectators will support, generating revenue, and maintaining legal compliance are largely incommensurable. This article calls into question the viability of UEFA's Financial Fair Play regulations and explores potential legal challenges to them under current EU law on the grounds of 1) restriction of competition, 2) abuse of a dominant position, and 3) restricted movement of workers. This chapter concludes with a discussion of possible alternatives to successfully addressing overspending and economic instability issues in European football. It is argued in this paper that EU law could serve as a tool for European football clubs to remedy issues associated with UEFA's FFP regulations that would help to create the conditions by which teams, beyond the well-established few, can remain competitive on the field and reap the economic benefits of on-field success.

LEGAL CHALLENGES TO FINANCIAL FAIR PLAY RULES

UEFA's FFP regulations are ripe for, and will likely to be the source of, many legal challenges through the violation of EU law. It is now well established that that EU law applies to the context of sport as an economic activity (see *URBSFA v. Bosman*, 1995).[13] There are clear differences between sport and traditional business activities, however the European Commission's White Paper on Sport states that these differences "will continue to be recognised, but it cannot be construed so as to justify a general exemption from the application of EU law" (Commission, 2007, p. 1). Not all UEFA clubs are in member states of the EU; however, there are at least twenty-seven clubs that are. As such, it is not possible for UEFA to operate outside of EU law.

The following section examines three possible EU legal challenges to FFP regulations that European football clubs could make on the grounds of: 1) Article 101 of the Treaty on the Functioning of the European Union (TFEU), which prohibits anticompetitive agreements, 2) Article 102 of the TFEU, which prohibits abuse of a dominant position, and 3) Article 45 of the TFEU, which prohibits restrictions on the movement of workers between member states.

Restriction of Competition

Article 101 of the TFEU forbids "all agreements between undertakings, decisions by associations of undertakings and concerted practices which may affect trade between Member States and which have as their object or effect the prevention, restriction or

---

[13] See footnote 4 on page 15 for further details on the case.

distortion of competition within the internal market" (Treaty, 2007). Long (2012) argues that UEFA is an association of undertakings and that FFP regulations will affect trade. He argues further that an effect of FFP regulations is preserving the status quo by keeping financially well-off teams in financially well-off positions and creating barriers for advancement of other teams. There can be little doubt that the FFP regulations favour leading clubs with high football revenues by ensuring that they remain in powerful, profitable positions. This arrangement is economically anticompetitive.

Teams can challenge the regulations if they are excluded from UEFA competitions and lose revenue as a result. The European Court of Justice has allowed for some sporting exemption of access to competition on the basis of integrity of sport, e.g. *Meca-Medina*,[14] which is a sports doping case; the courts, however, would be much less likely to allow for denial of access to competition on the basis of imposed economic sanction. Players can challenge the regulations if their salaries are reduced by the need for a club to break even. Football agents might also be able to successfully challenge the FFP regulations on the grounds that they are anticompetitive and lessen their earning potential.

In May 2013, a player agent Daniel Striani filed a lawsuit challenging the break-even provision arguing that it violates EU law, which prohibits the restriction of competition (Mestre, 2013). The European Commission rejected the complaint, but not because of the compatibility of FFP regulations and EU competition law. Striani's complaint was referred to a Brussels court. In the Brussels court, Striani argued that the FFP regulations deflated player salaries, which in turn deflated player agent salaries. The Brussels court ruled that they did not have jurisdiction over UEFA and that Striani's financial losses were indirect; they did, however, grant Striani's request to block UEFA from proceeding with its next phase of FFP regulations, which would further limit the deficits clubs could incur. UEFA has appealed the decision, which has temporarily suspended the ruling until the appeal is heard, which has allowed UEFA to continue rolling out their FFP regulations. While the Striani legal challenges have not yet resulted in a clear ruling on the compatibility of FFP regulations with EU law, this is largely a result of jurisdictional issues rather than the legal merits of his arguments.

Abuse of a Dominant Position

Daniel Striani's complaint also alleged that FFP regulations are a violation of Article 102 of the TFEU, which prohibits abuse of a dominant position. Succeeding on these grounds would require establishing that UEFA is in a dominant position, and that it has committed abuse. UEFA is very clearly in a dominant position as the official union of football associations across Europe. Even in the case of FFP regulations that only apply to clubs who are participating or wish to participate in UEFA competitions, the pyramid structure of sports governance in Europe means that lower governing bodies have and will adopt similar regulations. For example, England has passed its

---

[14] See footnote 12 on page 16 for further details on the case.

own version of FFP rules that are applicable to all English clubs whether or not they wish to compete in UEFA competitions. This clearly establishes that UEFA has a distinct position of power over the multi-billion European football industry, and can instigate a trickle-down effect impacting clubs throughout Europe. The question then is, in establishing FFP regulations, has UEFA "abused" its power?

The conditions of abuse in Article 102 of the TFEU (2007) are specified as follows:

a) directly or indirectly imposing unfair purchase or selling prices or other unfair trading conditions;
b) limiting production, markets or technical development to the prejudice of consumers;
c) applying dissimilar conditions to equivalent transactions with other trading parties, thereby placing them at a competitive disadvantage;
d) making the conclusion of contracts subject to acceptance by the other parties of supplementary obligations which, by their nature or according to commercial usage, have no connection with the subject of such contracts.

FFP regulations arguably violate all of these conditions. Condition C is particularly important, as it has been well documented that the FFP regulations promote conditions that give well-established, wealthier clubs a competitive advantage on the field and in their potential to generate revenue. FFP regulations simultaneously disadvantage teams who are not yet well established. Or, as Hornsby (2011) puts it, "the break rule applies discriminatory rules to access to an 'essential facility' by raising barriers to entry that did not apply to those making the rules" (p. 5). Only a select group of leading clubs were involved in creating the FFP regulations that keep those same clubs at the top. Hornsby (2011) refers to these clubs as the "magic circle" (p. 5). Arguably, UEFA has abused their dominant position in developing and implementing their current FFP regulations.

Restricted Movement of Workers

Article 45 of the TFEU guarantees the fundamental right of free movement of workers between member states. In the aftermath of *Bosman* (1995) and other subsequent legal cases, it is quite clear that the European Court of Justice takes an open view towards protecting the free movement of athlete-workers in sport. The FFP regulations will affect the free movement of workers between member states. To provide one example, French President Francois Hollande has proposed a 75 percent income tax on salaries that exceed €1 million, to be paid by the company of the employee (Hollande, 2013). If this proposal was to pass, French football clubs would struggle to pay players competitive wages without potentially running deficits beyond FFP regulations. The result is that highly talented football players will be constrained in their ability to play for clubs in France.

Mestre (2013) argues that while TFEU Article 45 challenges are commonly discussed, they are highly unlikely to succeed. There can be no doubt that player movement will be affected by salary expenditure restrictions that clubs will face under FFP regulations. In contrast to dominant views amongst many lawyers and legal scholars, Mestre maintains that these restrictions are modest and even if teams fold or have no money for salaries, other teams in a country will allow for the free movement of athlete-workers between Member States. Whether or not a TFEU Article 45 challenge would be successful is debatable, but it is a question that could cast further doubt on the legality of UEFA's FFP regulations.

ESTABLISHING NECESSITY, SUITABILITY, AND PROPORTIONALITY

While sport does not have immunity from EU law, it has been recognized in case law and various treatises as a unique economic activity that allows for some legal exemptions on a case-by-case basis, as discussed in Chapter 2. The application of EU law is somewhat flexible in the context of sport. Therefore, although FFP regulations might be seen as violating EU law, it does not necessarily mean that UEFA would not be granted an exemption. Furthermore, in relation to Article 101 of the TFEU on restricting competition, a possible exemption is written into the TFEU on the grounds of legitimacy and proportionality (Trimdas, 2006).

On the grounds of legitimacy, it is possible that UEFA would be able to successfully argue that FFP regulations seek a basic legitimate objective, i.e. to maintain the long-term health and financial stability of European football for the benefit of millions of people involved in the sport as spectators, participants, sponsors, administrators, and peripheral businesses. It can be shown, however, that despite rampant club overspending without profitable returns, European football has remained impeccably stable. For example, according to a study by Kuper and Szymanski (2009), of the eighty-eight Football League teams in 1923, eighty-five still remained as of the 2007–2008 season. That is, 97 percent of teams were still active over an eighty-five-year timespan, which is highly stable. Storm (2012) argues that this stability is largely a result of financial bailouts clubs receive, often from public dollars, as the public are socially, culturally, and emotionally tied to their football clubs. Likewise, Morrow (2013) suggests that team shareholders are typically not investing in clubs with financial profit-driven motives but rather, because they feel attached to clubs and feel a sense of obligation to support them. While this might not be an ideal economic model in a capitalist system, it has successfully worked for over 85 years. As such, it might be difficult for UEFA to argue that a legal exemption should be granted on the grounds that FFP regulations are a necessity.

Even if the aim of UEFA is perceived as legitimate and necessary by European courts, the way in which UEFA has set out to accomplish their aim may not be. In terms of actual suitability, the FFP regulations are not necessarily effective in accomplishing what they have set out to do. According to Kilb (2014), "there exist a variety of loopholes and workarounds that could allow teams to continue their extravagant spending, leaving the rules nothing more than additional work for accountants" (p. 808). Schubert (2014) calls into question the effectiveness of a deterrence based approach to shaping football club decision making. As football revenues increase so to do club expenditures on top-level talent. The objective of winning will likely continue to outweigh the objective of making profit, leading clubs to continue overspending leading to fines and heightened financial instability. Furthermore, Madden (2012) argues that compliance with FFP rules will also result in less financial stability in European football as they will reduce the quality of play and drive down ticket sales and broadcast revenue. Additionally, non-compliant top-level teams could eventually face exclusion from marquee competitions, resulting in lost revenues for everyone involved in European football.

Further to this, Szymanski (2012) identifies that teams rarely go into insolvency due to irrational or undisciplined financial spending, and that a decline in playing level and position typically precedes insolvency. Therefore, the break-even rule will not address the actual root cause of insolvency. Also, Hornsby (2014) finds that the corporate worth of "challenger" clubs will decrease dramatically as FFP regulations "place a ceiling on their ambition" (p. 1). FFP regulations do not address the primary causes of football's financial woes, and in fact heighten them particularly for less-established clubs. While UEFA might have legitimate aims, their FFP regulations might in fact worsen the situation that they are trying to remedy.

Ambition, growth, and success of less-established football clubs are essential to the stability of European football. The collapse of Rangers FC is often held up as an indication of the need for FFP regulations that ensure that football clubs do not suffer a similar fate, disrupting the stability of European football. Morrow (2015) argues that the over-development and commercialisation of a small number of clubs, and in the case of Scottish football two clubs, creates significant risks as the league becomes financially dependent on those clubs and their potential collapse threatens the stability of other clubs and the league. FFP regulations that serve to promote well-established, affluent clubs, while limiting ambition and growth of less-established, emerging clubs will present new economic risks by heightening the importance of a select group of clubs to the stability of European Football.

If the courts deem FFP regulations to be legitimate, UEFA must also show that they are proportionate; that is, that the regulations go no further than is necessary to achieve their objective (Trimdas, 2006). To prove this, UEFA would need to show that the FFP regulations are the least restrictive mechanism to remedy the financial crisis in European football. As will be outlined in the next section, there are many other approaches that UEFA could adopt that would be less restrictive. In light of these alternative approaches, FFP regulations are unlikely to pass the proportionality test.

ALTERNATIVE APPROACHES TO FINANCIAL FAIR PLAY RULES

There can be little doubt that a financial crisis has swept European football that has bankrupted some clubs and pushed the overall club deficit to over €1 billion. If UEFA's FFP regulations are not a viable answer to this crisis, the question then becomes: What is the best approach to fix football's financial follies?

Kilb (2014) argues that the most effective approach would be to "push the domestic league governing body in each of its 53 member states to introduce its own version of Financial Fair Play regulations" (p. 838). In so doing, legal challenges involving member states and EU law would be significantly diminished. This would also allow for countries to set their own viable guidelines within the constraints of their own contexts, e.g. taxation provisions. Furthermore, if the approach mirrored that used in England, all clubs would be involved in the ratification of the guidelines, rather than a select few, so it would be significantly less likely to be challenged. The challenge of this, however, would be getting all governing bodies to agree across each European country. Governing bodies that choose to opt out in a state-run model could hoard talented, highly-paid players and further increase talent gaps across teams in the continent. This approach also rests on the hypothesis that teams overspend on talented players to explain football deficits and insolvencies, which is not the complete picture of the financial situation and likely will not solve the financial issues. It is, however, preferable to the UEFA model because it is less prone to legal challenges.

Another approach could be to adopt the North American salary cap model. In an attempt to ensure long-term financial sustainability and competitive balance in the 1980s, major sports leagues in North America instituted salary cap systems (Bodansky, 2011). The salary caps have been aimed at ensuring that teams do not overspend on all-star calibre athletes' salaries, and that large-market teams that earn more profits are not able to buy winning talent while small-market teams struggle to field competitive teams. In the North American professional sports context, the salary cap system appears to work in providing financial stability and a measure of completive balance between large and small market teams.

A formal salary cap system would not, however, be practical in a European open-competition context (Lindholm, 2010). Leagues in North America are closed, with teams remaining the same from year to year with the rare exception of expansion teams. In contrast, European football associations operate on a promotion and relegation system whereby standings at the end of a season determine the level at which teams play in the following season. With teams moving to different divisions from year to year, it would be difficult to impose a salary cap on specific leagues. A uniform salary cap might be possible in theory, but in practice, it would need to appeal to the least economically viable team in a low-level division, which would drive down wages and invite legal challenges for violating EU competition law (Lindholm, 2010). The advantage of this model over FFP regulations is that it would simultaneously promote fiscal responsibility and competitive balance, which could foster spectator interest to drive up revenue without the ability for teams to misspend their revenue.

Another aspect of the North American commercial sports model is revenue sharing (Van Noll, 2014). The basic premise of revenue sharing is that all teams contribute to the financial stability of a sports league and it is therefore in the interests of all teams to ensure that revenue is shared. This approach helps to promote competitive balance between large and small-market teams, as well as ensuring that no teams run into insurmountable financial hardships. This could be challenged under anticompetitive provisions of EU law. However, the White Paper has established that sport is a unique economic activity, and the benefit of seeing competitive organizations succeed financially is one of those unique aspects. In other realms of a capitalist economy, it would be quite rare for an organization to benefit from the financial success of their competitors. As such, revenue sharing could likely be justified by UEFA and would be a less invasive approach than FFP regulations. There is revenue sharing built into current FFP regulations, whereby fines for not breaking even are distributed among clubs that are financially sound. This model is based on the flawed approach of stealing from the poor to pay the wealthy. It is more logical for the wealthy to share with the poor to ensure the continued sustainability of the enterprise by which they make their wealth.

Kehrli (2014) puts forward an argument for a much less invasive approach to fixing the financial woes of European football clubs, which would simply be to hire a large team of UEFA certified financial experts. Clubs who run deficits would then voluntarily have a UEFA financial expert assigned to their club to provide guidance on responsible spending. Schubert (2014) makes a similar argument, suggesting that heightened guidance and education are a necessity to promoting better financial decision-making by football clubs, rather than a punitive approach adopted in the FFP regulations. Kehrli (2014) also suggests that a reward system could be put in place. Instead of punishing teams for non-compliance and creating increased financial and competitive barriers for clubs that are struggling financially, Kehrli (2014) suggests that teams could be rewarded for compliance.

Another approach would be for UEFA to place less financial benefit on winning by reducing or eliminating prize money. In 2012–2013, FC Bayern Munich was awarded over €55 million in prize money for winning the Champion's League. Financial incentives like this are likely at the heart of club over-expenditures. Money is already significantly tied to winning through spectator interest and the revenues that come with it, e.g. ticket sales, apparel proceeds, broadcast revenue, etc. Prize money adds further pressure on football clubs to take financial risks and gambles in the hopes of a pay-off. A significant advantage of this approach is that there are not obvious legal challenges to it.

A multifaceted approach that adopts elements of these strategies could be much more effective in fixing the financial issues that plague European football. A multifaceted approach would also stand the test of time without falling to eventual legal challenges. Prize money could be limited, so that money could instead be used to employ UEFA financial experts to provide guidance to clubs, and increased revenue sharing could be implemented in the interests of all clubs. This would more effectively achieve UEFA's aims and place less restrictions than the FFP regulations. Teams would have the possibility of fielding a competitive squad and securing the economic benefits of on-field success.

Conclusion

The goal of UEFA in developing FFP regulations is the long-term financial stability of European football. Though highly complex in its details, the main purpose of the regulations are to provide constraints on club deficit spending to ensure that teams do not fold or enter financial disrepute, e.g. not paying employees. Despite their intended purpose, the FFP regulations will not be effective in achieving stable finances in European football. The regulations will not work to prevent bankruptcies, as overspending is not solely responsible for the financial difficulties and deficits faced by countless football clubs. The rules might also have the unintended consequence of diminishing the level of play, lowering the revenues generated in European football, and creating further financial issues for football clubs to grapple with.

This chapter has shown that the FFP regulations contravene EU law. Lawsuits, like those brought forward by FIFA agent Daniel Striani, will add new costs for clubs and UEFA to incur, hurt the public image of European football, and could lead to a lack of enforcement of the rules for fear of legal repercussions. In 2014, UEFA reached settlements with at least nine clubs, rather than imposing sanctions, in what was likely a means to avoid further lawsuits. It is as Hornsby predicted in his 2011 statement, "UEFA is between a rock and hard place. The harder the law, the more its legality will be questioned. The softer it undoubtedly is means the less effective it will be" (p. 3). UEFA is now faced with the prospect of enforcing sanctions and facing legal challenges or loosening their restrictive sanctions, which will make their strategy even less effective.

While something should be done to remedy the ever-increasing deficits of European football clubs, FFP regulations are not likely to be a viable solution. Clubs can turn to the law to have the FFP rules struck down. FFP regulations will not only be ineffective, they will end up thrusting European football into a greater financial crisis. Other less restrictive and more effective strategies should be considered for fixing the financial follies of European football that allow teams the opportunity to successfully meet their economic and on-field performance objectives.

CHAPTER 5

Bloodsport: Violence and Criminal Law in British Rugby

INTRODUCTION

Sports and violence have been deeply connected throughout human history. The term arena, which is so central to many sports, derives from the ancient Roman tradition of spreading harena, or sand, to soak up the blood of competitors (Katz, 1996). In the modern era, violence and aggression remain prerequisites for success in many sports such as boxing, ice hockey, gridiron football, lacrosse, and rugby. Despite a long history of violence in sport, the role of the law and criminal courts in responding to and mitigating such violence has long been unclear and inconsistent. This chapter uses rugby violence in the UK, including both Rugby League and Rugby Union, as a window into the ways in which violence in sport can become legal matters, as British rugby has significant case law pertaining to sports violence. In contrast, the violent sport of Canadian football has no criminal case law related to it at present (Fogel, 2013). The aims of this chapter are to: i) examine what rugby violence is and why it occurs, ii) trace the history of legal intervention into rugby violence in the UK, and iii) identify controversial issues in prosecuting rugby violence and establishing a threshold of criminality.

Few sports combine the speed, physicality, and person-on-person collisions with minimal protective equipment that are featured in rugby. While established norms and rules are in place to ensure a measure of safety on the pitch, excessive violence continues to plague the sport. Rugby violence can lead to serious long-term injuries for athletes and the occasional death on the pitch, in addition to other serious social problems. This chapter provides a socio-legal analysis of why excessive rugby violence occurs as well as the consequences of such violence. Twenty-one criminal prosecutions in the UK for alleged thuggery on the pitch are examined, and the unique challenges of prosecuting rugby violence are identified including issues related to unclear laws, establishing actus reus and mens rea, discerning consent, and maintaining public interests. Arguments and specifications for the establishment of a clear, research-informed, and balanced sports-violence criminalization threshold test are discussed.

The use of the courts and criminal law for on-field violence is relatively rare, considering that "each year, millions of people are injured whilst playing sport" (Fafinski, 2005, p. 414). Violence is an integral part of many sports, and many sports could not continue as they are currently structured without elements of violence. The judge in *Henderson*[15] (1976) reaffirms this point by stating, "I fully realize that if too

---

[15] Henderson, an ice hockey player, was charged with assault for a violent, on-ice act.

many legal restrictions are placed upon those who participate in sports where the very nature of the game precipitates bodily contact, the game will soon lose not only players but also spectators" (p. 127).

Smith (1987) contends that beyond maintaining the integrity of certain sports, there are several other reasons for why the criminal courts have given the arena of sport relative immunity. First, he suggests that the police and courts have other priorities to focus on, like murders and robberies. Second, sports leagues have internal player control mechanisms that could be potentially more effective in dealing with such matters. Third, civil law proceedings have been well established as an option for injured players to proceed with their grievances. Fourth, it could be perceived as unfair to criminalise the individual player while ignoring those who have guided or coached players into violent acts, such as the team captain or coach. Fifth, it would be unfair to criminalise a player when the law has been so unclear about what is and is not seen to be reasonable on-field violence. Sixth, it is very difficult to reach a guilty verdict in cases involving on-field violence, due to several challenges that will be discussed later in this chapter. And seventh, prosecuting athletes does very little to address and solve the problem of sports violence and the injuries that result. While his list is extensive, one aspect that Smith does not mention is that sportspersons appear unlikely to come forward to police with criminal complaints for injuries they have sustained during play, which makes investigations and subsequent prosecutions unlikely.

On rare occasions, cases of on-field violence do cross over an undefined threshold of criminality and are deemed to be criminal violence. Many legal scholars have argued that this is problematic and that the courts should restrain from getting involved in cases of on-field violence (Gardiner, 1994; Gardiner & Felix, 1995; Gardiner & James, 1997; Standen, 2009). Summarising this position, Gardiner and Felix (1995) state "better a man with a whistle regulating the game than a man with a wig!" (p. 213). Others argue that the criminal law must have a central role in cases of on-field violence to curb increasing occurrences of injurious violence, protect players, avoid bringing sports into disrepute, and to have an educating effect on sports participants to fully know and understand the limits of acceptable body contact (Blackshaw, 2008; Grayson, 1971, 1988, 1990, 1994, 1999; Grayson & Bond, 1993).

My argument in this chapter is that a middle ground must be established in which better and more transparent self-regulation is encouraged alongside a more clearly defined threshold for the intervention of criminal law. Furthermore, legal and disciplinary mechanisms alone will not eradicate all problems associated with rugby violence. A more multi-faceted prevention approach that rests on education initiatives for players and coaches, support networks, and heightened research and awareness of the problems associated with rugby violence is required.

UNDERSTANDING VIOLENCE IN RUGBY

Outside the realm of contact sports, violence is often understood to be illegal, disdainful, force that should not be tolerated. Within the realm of contact sports, however, conceptions of violence are much more complicated as some acts of violence might be celebrated as feats of strength, masculinity, and athletic superiority, while other acts might violate the unique norms of sporting violence and be sanctioned severely. There is some debate on whether or not sports like rugby are becoming increasingly violent. For example, Dunning (1999) traces the history of sports violence and argues that sports violence has been in decline, while Leizman (1999) argues the very opposite, suggesting that acts of excessive violence in sport are rising dramatically. Regardless of which argument is adopted, there is no denying that sports violence has long been an important social issue and continues to remain a social problem.

Before entering into a discussion on the legal aspects of excessive rugby violence, it is important to take a step back to conceptualize the following: i) how violence and aggression are defined in this work, ii) what the different forms of sports violence that occur during play are, and iii) why excessive violence occurs in rugby.

Conceptualizing Violence in Sport

The online Oxford Dictionary defines violence as "Behaviour involving physical force intended to hurt, damage, or kill someone or something." By using this definition, two main characteristics of violence can be identified: i) physical force, and ii) intent to harm. This definition is challenging to apply to the context of sport as arguably, the normative actions in many sports are to harm an opponent through physical force. For example, a boxer punches an opponent, often in the face and head, with a goal of knocking the fighter out of consciousness to secure a win. If the online Oxford Dictionary definition of violence is assumed to be valid, it could then be argued that sports like boxing and rugby are inherently violent by their very structure, rules, objectives, and norms.

Many sociologists and philosophers of sport have pointed out that violence can be contextual, and that what is deemed violence in one social context is not necessarily considered to be violence in another (Atyeo, 1981; Coakley and Donnelly, 2004, 2009; Leizman, 1999; Smith 1983). Furthermore, athletes themselves often do not define the acts of physical contact that occur on the field as violence, even though they would define similar acts as violence if they occurred off of the field (Fogel, 2013). For example, a routine rugby tackle that occurs during play is typically not defined as violence by those who play the sport, while if a similar tackle occurred while someone was walking on a sidewalk on their way to work it would be defined as violent. The act of the tackle is the same, but the context shapes whether or not it is defined as violence. As such, it is necessary to define violence within the context of rugby, taking into account the culture, norms, and objectives of the sport. For the purposes of this chapter, rugby violence will be defined as excessive physical force that violates the norms and rules of the game, and causes or has the potential to cause physical harm.

Smith (1983) has argued that on-field violence exists on a continuum that includes: i) brutal body contact, ii) borderline violence, iii) quasi-criminal violence, and iv) criminal violence. *Brutal body contact* is characterized as common physical contact that occurs in certain sports, is expected, and sometimes results in injuries. An example of brutal body contact is a body check in men's ice hockey. Outside the context of specific sports this contact could be defined as criminal assault, but within the sport it is not criminal or unlawful. *Borderline violence* is characterized by physical contact that violates the rules of the game but is accepted by most players and coaches as being within the norms of the sport. An example of borderline violence would be a deliberate foul on a poor free throw shooter in the sport of basketball which is often done to stop the game clock and allow a team to regain possession of the ball with a low risk of giving up two or three points. Though in violation of the rules, borderline violence is an expected, strategic component of competitive sport. Borderline violence is often punished in a game by a referee or official, but such acts are not defined as criminal. *Quasi-criminal violence* is characterized by violations of the formal rules of the game, public laws, and playing norms. Serious injuries often result from such acts. Players, coaches, and spectators usually condemn such acts, and fines and suspensions are usually imposed on the player who committed the violent act. An example of quasi-criminal violence would be a baseball player storming the mound and throwing a punch at the pitcher who had hit him with an errant pitch. The courts allow the governing bodies of sport to impose their own sanctions on quasi-criminal violence and do not intervene. *Criminal violence* is characterized by actions that are in violation of formal rules of the game, public laws, and the norms of a sport. Such actions result in serious bodily injury or death. An example of criminal violence in sport would be a rugby player deliberately picking up an opposing player and driving them head down into the ground in what can be termed a pile-driver maneuver. This violence is widely condemned in sport and leads to prosecution of such acts under criminal law (Smith, 1983).

While useful in identifying a continuum of violence in sport, Smith's (1983) typology relies heavily on the reaction to particular acts and the labels that are subsequently attached to determine different types of violence. This is problematic in that it assumes a consistency in reactions and labels, suggesting that referees, governing bodies of sport, and criminal justice systems are consistent in their responses to violence in sport. It is my contention that the labeling of violence is highly contextual, economic, and political, and that an adequate typology of violence in sport should hinge on action, intent, harm, and consent, rather than reactions and labels. Adjusting Smith's typology, I argue that there are three main types of physical contact in sport: (a) routine contact, (b) immoderate violence, and (c) ultra-violence (Fogel, 2013). *Routine contact* is authorised by the rules of sport, common, deemed consensual by the majority of athletes, and causes minimal or no injury e.g. a routine tackle. *Immoderate violence* is unauthorised in the rules of sport, non-consensual yet relatively common, and not so extreme that legal officials become involved, e.g. pushing a player from behind. *Ultra-violence, or "thuggery"* is an extreme form of violence that is unauthorised, non-consensual, committed with recklessness or intent to harm, and causes severe injury, e.g. a player using his cleats to stomp on the head of an opposing player (such as the case in *R v. Lloyd*, 1989). It is this third category of physical contact, ultra-violence/thuggery that is the focus of this research on rugby violence.

Explanations for Rugby Violence

Rugby violence can be explained from a range of disciplinary and theoretical perspectives. As with any human behaviour, no single theory is adept at explaining why all people act or fail to act in particular ways. Likewise, it is an impossible task to separate out the biological, psychological, and physiological aspects of human behaviour, such as violence in rugby, from social, cultural, political, and commercial aspects of human existence. In this chapter no attempt is made to establish a grand theory of rugby violence that can explain all cases. Instead, an attempt is made to outline and understand some of the natural and social forces that push and pull rugby players in the direction of committing acts of ultra-violence on the pitch. Having some understanding of why rugby players commit such violent acts is integral to the task of effectively remedying and preventing the harmful consequences of rugby violence.

Biologically Determined Aggression

From a biological perspective, aggression is an innate human characteristic. Instinct theorists, such as Lorenz (1963), posit that aggression is an instinct that is essential to human survival, and violence in sport serves as a means to release this innate instinct. Freud (1922) proposed that aggressive instincts or impulses are found in the subconscious "ID," and that humans will act aggressively unless reined in by their "Superego." Freud believed that one particular instinct is the "death drive" that pushes people to destroy and kill. This death instinct must then be vented to, through a process known as catharsis, to prevent continuous act of random violence. Violent sports like rugby could be perceived as cathartic, allowing for the venting of aggressive impulses. Dollard et al. (1939) contended that aggression is an innate response to frustrating situations, and that frustration will always produce some form of aggression. This view is often termed Frustration-Aggression Theory. Frustration in a rugby game can involve being unable to achieve a particular outcome, such as advancing the ball, being subject to a referee's perceived poor call, or losing a game.

Contemporary biological theories of aggression argue that violence results from brain, chromosomal, and/or hormonal abnormalities. A meta-analysis of 43 brain-imaging studies showed significantly reduced prefrontal brain function in individuals with violent behaviors (Yang & Raine, 2009). Similarly, Leutgeb et al. (2015) compared brain-imaging data of violent offenders to non-offenders and also found significantly reduced prefrontal brain function. The notion that chromosomal abnormality, specifically the presence of an extra Y chromosome in men, or what is sometimes called XYY syndrome, has long fascinated scientists and the general public. In the 1960s, it was widely believed that men with an extra Y chromosome were likely to be violent and aggressive as a result of the extra male sex chromosome. Many subsequent studies have shown that this is not the case, although some contemporary researchers continue to argue that a significant relationship between XYY and aggression exist (Stochholm et al., 2012). The most common biological explanation of aggression is as a result of hormones—testosterone in particular.

Bateup et al. (2002) studied this link between testosterone and aggression in the context of women's rugby. In their study, they conducted saliva tests on 17 adult female rugby players 24 hours before competitions, 20 minutes before competitions, and immediately after competitions. They found that testosterone levels continued to increase leading up to and during competition. The results suggest a link between testosterone and participation in an aggressive sport, but they do not show the direction of the correlation, as it could be that participation in the sport increases testosterone rather than an increase in testosterone leads individuals to partake in violent activities.

Biological theories of aggression appear inconclusive on the role instincts, impulses, brain abnormalities, chromosomes, and hormones play in acts of extreme violence in sports like rugby. There may be some biological basis of aggression, but there is also very clearly a role that social, cultural, political, and commercial forces also play in shaping violent behaviour on the pitch, which must also be considered.

Social Learning of Violence

The origins of Social Learning Theory are in the work of Tarde (1912) who proposed that deviant behaviors are learned through contact with others and imitation of superiors. Sutherland (1947) furthered this conception of learning by proposing that individuals learn the values, attitudes, beliefs, rationalizations, motivations, and techniques of deviant and criminal behaviour through social interaction in intimate personal groups. Burgess and Akers' (1966) built on Sutherland's work by incorporating principles of operant conditioning and reinforcement. Likewise, Bandura (1971, 1973, 1977, 1978) looked specifically at how violence and aggression are the result of learned behaviour through observation and imitation. Social Learning Theory draws significantly from the concept of modeling, whereby learning occurs by observing the behaviour of others, as well as the rewards and punishments that result from those behaviours.

For Bandura (1971) "observed rewards and punishments can play an important role in regulating behaviour" (p. 229). Bandura referred to the concept of learning through observation of rewards and punishments as "vicarious reinforcement" (p. 228). Bandura's theorizing was derived from experiments he conducted at Stanford University, the most famous being his Bobo Doll experiments. In his Bobo Doll experiments Bandura measured children's behavior after watching a model receive rewards, punishments, or no consequences for aggressive and non-aggressive acts against an inflatable Bobo Doll. Bandura found that children exposed to aggressive acts against the Bobo Doll were more likely to act in physically aggressive ways, particularly if no punishment followed the aggressive behavior of the model.

Social Learning Theory has been used to explain violence and other deviant behaviour in rugby. In a 2004 study, Muir and Seitz observed over 50 male collegiate rugby teams in the United States in both competitive and non-competitive contexts over a four-year period. They found that through interaction among themselves and with other rugby players, and through observations of more senior players by first-year collegiate rugby players, that unique values, norms, and behaviours were learned and perpetuated. According to Muir and Seitz (2004), "these behaviors, whether occurring in competitive or non-competitive environments, functioned to provide the players with a sense of belonging, unity, and purpose within the context of the subculture" (p. 322). Violence, aggression, and other potentially criminal and deviant acts can be learned by rugby players through interactions, observations, and perceived rewards for such behaviours.

Violent Masculine Identity Formation and Maintenance

A significant aspect of the socialization processes that occur in sport is directed towards masculine identity formation and maintenance. Characteristics seen to be feminine, weak, or soft are treated with contempt in the highly misogynistic and homophobic world of competitive men's sports (see Forbes et al., 2006). Male athletes are socialized to aspire towards masculine identities that exude toughness, strength, power, and dominance. This is understood as part of the blueprint for assembling competitive athletes and winning teams. Messner (1992) makes the important observation that not only is sport an arena where violent, dominant forms of masculinity are taught to boys and young men, but that sport is an arena where constant masculinity struggles between men occur. He argues, "sport must be viewed as an institution through which domination is not only imposed, but also contested; an institution within which power is constantly at play" (p. 13).

Connell and Messerschmidt (2005) assert that masculinities are part of a highly complex gender hierarchy. There are hierarchies of masculinities within social institutions, characterized by complex power struggles, with dominant and subordinate forms. Masculinities are "multiple" with power relations of gender operating between men, particularly in the context of male-oriented total institutions (Carrigan, Connell, & Lee, 1985, p. 551). Competitive rugby is an arena for masculinity contests, power relations, and dominance. This, in turn, can lead to a high risk for the occurrence of violence as an integral part of performing masculinity.

Messner (2002) characterizes the "athletic masculinity" that is constructed in sport as dangerous, leading to what he terms "the triad of violence" whereby masculine ideals lead athletes to commit violence against opponents, against themselves in the form of playing through injuries, and against women in the form of sexual and physical violence (p. 27). Masculinity becomes a competition within sport, where these three forms of violence become mechanisms by which male athletes climb the rungs of the hierarchy of athletic masculinity.

It is my view that the competition for masculine identity acknowledgment and dominance is particularly dangerous in the context of sport because of the precariousness of athletic or sporting masculinities. Masculine status in sports is highly unstable and constantly under threat, requiring continued identity work. An athlete might have a poor performance on the field of play, receive condemnation from the crowd and coaches, and be shunned by teammates, even if a few days earlier the athlete hit a game-winning shot and was celebrated as a hero by coaches, teammates, and fans. Likewise, injuries can take athletes out of athletic competitions and have the potential to end their athletic careers in an instant. This notion is expressed well by a junior Canadian football players I interviewed in a previous study who stated, "we are all aware of the potential that your career could be over [with] the next snap because some guy rolls up on you from behind and you blow every ligament in your knee" (Fogel, 2013, p. 39). Their masculine status is highly unstable and precarious. This precariousness of masculinity has dangerous implications, as some male athletes may engage in harmful behaviours, such as thuggery on the field, to stabilize their masculine dominance.

Rugby Violence as Tolerable Positive Deviance

The term "deviance" refers to a deviation from the norm or the average. Criminologists and sociologists have traditionally associated the term deviance as being a negative act because an individual fails to abide by a rule or rules, which can elicit a negative reaction from others. For Howard (1963) deviance has two main characteristics: i) a violation of a norm, and ii) a negative societal reaction to that norm violation. The term deviance can be thought of in a mathematical sense, as standards of "deviation" away from a mean or average. Deviant acts are those that are not average or normal; deviants are statistical outliers.

A component that has been missing in many traditional descriptions and understandings of deviance is that breaking a norm or deviating from the average does not necessarily mean that an individual has failed to follow a norm or has fallen short of average. As Hughes and Coakley (1991) contend, deviance can also result from over-conforming to norms and going well beyond average. Deviance in sport can, and often does, result from over-conformity to social norms or what Hughes and Coakley (1991) term the "sports ethic" (p. 307). Providing a detailed illustration, Coakley and Donnelly (2004) write,

> If a football player were to deliver a punishing tackle, which broke the ribs or destroyed the kidney of an opposing running back after his coach had told him to be aggressive and to put his body on the line for the team, the violence would be based on extreme conformity to norms. Such violence is "part of the job," and it would be seen as justified by most fans, highlighted on television replays, and respected by teammates and even many opponents. The player would feel righteous in his actions, despite their harmful consequences, and he would be prepared to do them again, even if it meant doing harm to his own body or the bodies of others. (p. 188)

This type of deviance resulting from over-conformity can be referred to as "positive deviance" (Coakley and Donnelly, 2004, p. 307).

Positive deviance in sport is widespread with pervasive sentiments of winning at all costs, constant striving for improvement and excellence, and the never-ending quest to be the best. These are the norms of sport; they are the expected behaviours. According to Coakley (2008), over-conforming to these norms, the sport ethic, results in a range of deviance behaviours committed by athletes in sport such as playing through horrific injuries, using performance-enhancing drugs, and resorting to extreme violence on the field. Coakley (2008) writes that athletes "often take extreme measures to prove themselves, even if it involves violence. Violence reinforces feelings of self-worth by inviting affirmation from other athletes" (p. 200).

While positive deviance resulting from over-conformity to the sport ethic is often celebrated in some sports, particularly violent acts in a sport like rugby may lead to consequences that are devastatingly serious when these acts go too far. However, violence in rugby is typically tolerated as an expected part of the sport, and acts of extreme violence are often accepted as a by-product of the rugby ethic of aggression, violence, and winning at all costs. Sheard and Dunning (1973) note that rugby subculture allows players: "to behave with impunity in a manner which would bring immediate condemnation and punishment were it to occur among other social strata." Violence in rugby is promoted, it is tolerated, it is part of the sport ethic, and rugby players continue to engage in it with minimal public disdain or intervention from the law.

Commercialization of Sports Violence

Some athletes receive significant financial compensation for their violent acts on the fields of play. Violence is their job. This incentive exists within the context of rugby, where a player who is more aggressive will often have a higher likelihood of earning more playing time, advancing to higher playing levels, and having the opportunity to earn money playing the sport. With the rise in popularity of the Ultimate Fighting Championships and other commodified forms of sports violence, it seems quite obvious that sports violence sells.

Existing research on sports violence and spectatorship suggests that fans like to see violence in sports (Bryant, Cominsky, & Zillman, 1977; Bryant, Comisky, & Zillman, 1981; Bryant et al., 1982; Goldstein, 1998; Hauge, 2012; Jewell, 2012). Bryant et al. (1977, 1981, 1982) argue that the media exploit this yearning for violence. One way in which this is done is through over-coverage of violent plays. For example, violent acts in sport are often sensationalized and replayed in slow motion to prolong the violence and allow for each detail to be witnessed. Likewise, television advertisements often draw on past acts of violence from previous sport contests to encourage fans to watch upcoming events. According to Young and Smith (1988), slow motion and instant replay have been used to increase the media coverage of violence on the field. When violent hits happen live, they occur so fast that a viewer can miss them. With slow motion replay, viewers can see each violent tackle and examine the intricacies of the hit, as well as the injuries that often occur.

Violence sells in the competitive commercial world of sport. Violence is an important part of the show or product that television programs and league owners and administrators are selling to potential customers who watch sporting events and attend games. This financial imperative of violence in sport provides an incentive for governing bodies of sport to overlook and tolerate violent acts on the pitch, as well as to provide financial rewards to those athletes who are violent and aggressive. Hutchins and Phillips (1998) refer to this as "selling permissible violence" (p. 246).

An Integrated Theory of Rugby Violence

Violence in rugby is expected and tolerated for the most part. Tolerating violence in rugby serves the interests of fans who want to consume permissible violence, team managers who sell players and the violence they commit as commodities, and league officials whose jobs rest on the economic success of the leagues. In the sport of rugby, men are socialized to understand on-field violence as masculine and they are often rewarded with praise, playing time, and financial incentives for engaging in aggressive play. This violence is in turn tolerated and promoted as "permissible violence" (Hutchins & Phillips, 1998). It is difficult to determine exactly what role biology plays in shaping the aggressive play of athletes, but what is clear is that there are social forces related to masculine socialization and the commercial aspects of sport that continue to drive athletes towards violence and allow for the tolerance of such acts that would otherwise be disdainful, criminal conduct outside of the pitch.

Consequences of Rugby Violence

Excessive violence on the pitch has harmful consequences. Rugby violence can lead to bone fractures, torn muscles, spinal injuries, paralysis, and even death. In a previous study, media reports of 44 incidents of rugby players dying from rugby-related injuries were found, three of which resulted in criminal convictions (Sine and Fogel, 2013). Rugby participants already have a higher than average risk of injury compared with participants of other common team sports (Brown et al., 2015). In fact, rugby ranks among the most fatal team sports, with high incident rates of spinal and brain injuries (Fuller, 2008). According to Young (1993), sport is a:

> Hazardous workplace, replete with its unique forms of industrial disease. No other single milieu, including the risky and labour-intensive settings of miners, oil drillers or construction site workers can compare with the routine injuries of team sports such as football, ice hockey, rugby and the like (p. 373).

Violent acts that go beyond the limits of an already violent sport are especially dangerous in the context of rugby.

Beyond immediate and often catastrophic personal harms, there are considerable economic costs associated with sports injuries. A now-dated Australian study estimated that over $1 billion per year is spent in the country on medical costs for sports injuries; of those, of which the most common were from rugby (Egger, 1990). Young and White (2000) estimate that sports injuries cause workers to miss 11.5 million working days per year in England and Wales at a cost of £575 million. Yang et al. (2007) estimate that the Emergency Room costs of treating sports injuries incurred by American youth to be $1.8 billion per year.

The pain of injuries sustained during play can be lifelong for athletes, and can contribute to other issues such as depression, dementia, substance abuse, and increased suicide risk (O'Connell & Manschreck, 2012; Romero, 2015). Sports violence can have a trickle-down effect whereby young athletes learn violence and dangerous play by watching older players play in such a fashion, thus perpetuating excessive violence on the pitch from generation to generation (Leizman, 1999).

Furthermore, excessive on-field violence can be linked to crowd violence and public rioting. For example, in the 1924 Olympic rugby union final in France between the United States and France, an American player made a hard tackle on a French player leaving him to be carried off the field unconscious and covered in blood. The crowd began to riot and violence broke out between spectators. Spectators also threw items on the field, in one instance knocking an American player unconscious. The American team had to be escorted off of the field by French police (Rugby Football History, 2015).

RUGBY VIOLENCE PROSECUTIONS IN THE UK

Despite high injury incidence rates and high medical costs associated with rugby violence, criminal prosecutions are not overly common. On occasion, however, the courts do interfere in the on-field happenings of violence in British rugby. The following chart depicts a chronological history of all of the cases that were located:

Name	Year	Ball	Charge	Outcome
Billinghurst	1978	Off	Grievous bodily harm	Guilty
Gingell	1980	Off	Grievous bodily harm	Plead Guilty
Johnson	1986	Off	Grievous bodily harm	Guilty
Bishop	1986	Off	Common assault	Plead Guilty
Lloyd	1989	Off	Grievous bodily harm	Guilty
Rees	1992	Off	Grievous bodily harm	Acquitted
Marsh	1994	Off	Grievous bodily harm	Guilty
Hardy	1994	Off	Manslaughter	Acquitted
Collins	1994	Off	Grievous bodily harm	Guilty
Goodwin	1995	On	Grievous bodily harm	Guilty
Deverereux	1996	Off	Grievous bodily harm	Guilty
Calton	1998	Off	Grievous bodily harm	Plead Guilty
Moss	2000	Off	Grievous bodily harm	Guilty
Powell	2001	Off	Grievous bodily harm	Guilty
Bowyer	2002	Off	Grievous bodily harm	Guilty
Pepper	2002	Off	Assault occasioning harm	Guilty
Best	2004	Off	Assault occasioning harm	Guilty
Garfield	2007	Off	Unlawful wounding	Guilty
Evans	2010	Off	Assault occasioning harm	Acquitted
Unsworth	2013	Off	Unlawful wounding	Acquitted
O'Callaghan	2015	Off	Assault occasioning harm	Plead Guilty

While this list of 21 cases might appear to depict that prosecutions involving rugby violence are common, there are routinely one or less cases per year in England in a sport that over 250,000 people in England currently compete in, and is arguably the most violent popular team sport in the country (Sport England, 2015).

In the cases where criminal charges have been laid, very deliberate or reckless acts of violence on the pitch have resulted in severe injuries such as deep lacerations, permanent eye damage, and broken bones. For example, in *Garfield* (2007), the accused stomped on a player's head with his cleat causing a sizeable laceration. In *O'Callaghan* (2015), the accused kicked a player, who was on the ground, in the head, knocking him unconscious and breaking his jaw. The sound of the impact of his cleat striking the victim's face was reportedly so loud that it sounded as if a gunshot had been fired. In *Johnson* (1986), the accused bit the ear lobe off of an opposing player.

Issues Arising in Rugby Violence Prosecutions

While criminal convictions in rugby do happen, as no person or sport is above the law, the criminal courts remain somewhat unclear on exactly when and how they will determine if an act on the field of play should warrant criminal sanction or not, and remain largely reluctant to intervene in the happenings of rugby. In *Evans* (2010), the accused stomped on an opposing players head in a similar manner to the *Garfield* (2007) case, but yet he was acquitted. Extreme violence leading to injury in rugby is commonplace, and yet the courts rarely intervene. In this section I will examine the potential issues that arise in the prosecution of rugby violence. These issues relate to: i) unclear laws, ii) actus reus, iii) mens rea, iv) consent, and v) public interests.

Unclear Laws in the Context of Rugby

Sports violence is not specifically covered in English criminal law, and sport-specific precedents are both lacking and inconsistent. As such, there is no clear guidance to police, prosecutors, and judges as to how to proceed in cases of thuggery on the pitch. As is evidenced by the rugby prosecution chart, existing laws are at times applied to violent acts in rugby. The two most common charges are: 1) inflicting grievous bodily harm/unlawful wounding (GBH) and 2) assault occasioning actual bodily harm (ABH). Under Section 20 of the Offences Against the Person Act (1861), inflicting grievous bodily harm denotes causing serious bodily harm to another individual. Under section 47, assault occasioning actual bodily harm denotes causing bodily harm, but of a less serious nature than grievous bodily harm.

Applying these existing laws to the activities of a rugby pitch presents a challenge, as grievous and actual bodily harm are commonplace in the sport. In *Brown*[16] (1993), bodily harm was defined as follows:

---

[16] This is a non-sporting case that focused on the issue of consent in relation to violent and injurious sadomasochistic sexual acts involving a group of men.

> For this purpose, we think that "bodily harm" has its ordinary meaning and includes any hurt or injury calculated to interfere with the health or comfort of the prosecutor. Such hurt or injury need not be permanent, but must, no doubt, be more than merely transient and trifling (p. 230).

The Crown Prosecution Service (CPS, 2015) has gone further to specify that bodily harm includes any of the following: loss or breaking of a tooth or teeth, bruising, fracture of bones, or cuts requiring medical treatment. If every bruise, cut, or fracture were to result in criminal prosecutions, there would be 15 new cases after every rugby match. Fortunately, only those injuries that are very serious, and typically long-term, appear to be considered for possible criminal prosecution. In *Evans* (2010), though a player had their head stomped on by a cleat, the subsequent injuries were not deemed serious enough to warrant conviction. Where the precise threshold of injury or bodily harm is drawn remains unclear.

Establishing Actus Reus

In cases where serious, long-term bodily harm results, the prosecution is faced with a challenge of establishing actus reus. Establishing actus reus requires the prosecution to show that the accused was responsible for the act that has violated criminal law. This presents a challenge in the context of rugby where the action is fast-paced, body-contact is routine, and players are in very close-quarters with one another at times during the match. While increased use of filming of matches can provide some video evidence, they do not show what happens at the bottom of a pile of players.

For example, in *O'Callaghan* (2015), the accused allegedly bit off a portion of the ear of an opposing player while they were on the ground in a heap of players. The governing body of his league suspended him for two years for the act. In criminal court, however, he was acquitted as the burden of proof is higher in a criminal court than a disciplinary tribunal, and the prosecution was unable to definitively show that the ear was removed by O'Callaghan's mouth, rather than by other means such as a player stepping on it with a cleat. Definitively establishing actus reus in the context of rugby can be a challenge for the prosecution.

Establishing Mens Rea

Likewise, prosecutors must establish mens rea in concurrence with actus reus. Mens rea refers to the intention to commit an act that violates the law. In the case of inflicting grievous bodily harm, a lower threshold of mens rea is required, commonly referred to as recklessness. This requires showing that the accused recognized that an act would be dangerous and injury to another would likely result, and committed the act anyways.

Establishing mens rea in the context of rugby violence presents a challenge. On the one hand, it could be said that the intent of rugby players is to cause some bodily harm or hurt—though likely not of a serious nature—to their opponents in the pursuit of advancing the ball and winning matches. Again, if players were criminalized for this intent, countless criminal prosecutions would result after every match, and sports like boxing where the prime objective is to knock the other person unconscious through blows to their head would cease to exist. As Gunn (1998) argues, "the sport itself, and its rules, require the participants to act with the intention of inflicting harm to others" (p. 212).

Establishing recklessness is an even lower threshold. Qualitative research on sport (e.g. Fogel, 2013) reveals that athletes in high-contact sports understand their sport to be inherently risky, and that any one of their actions can cause serious harm or injury to opponents and, likewise, that at any moment they might be harmed by a serious, career-ending injury. While there are safety rules in sport intended to mitigate these risks, they do not remove all risk. When one rugby player tackles another to the ground during play, he or she intends to cause some hurt to the opponent and is aware that serious injury might result. Fortunately, the courts have almost consistently held that if an act, even if it is intentional and/or risky, is within the playing rules, that it should be exempt from criminal prosecution. This is directly acknowledged in the non-sports case of *Brown* (1993), where the judge stated:

> Some sports, such as the various codes of football, have deliberate bodily contact as an essential element. They lie at a mid-point between fighting, where the participant knows that his opponent will try to harm him, and the milder sports where there is at most an acknowledgement that someone may be accidentally hurt. In the contact sports each player knows and by taking part agrees that an opponent may from time to time inflict upon his body (for example by a rugby tackle) what would otherwise be a painful battery. By taking part he also assumes the risk that the deliberate contact may have unintended effects, conceivably of sufficient severity to amount to grievous bodily harm (p. 592).

This sporting exemption is also quite clear when looking at the rugby prosecutions chart on page 49, where all but one of the acts occurred away from the ball and were not part of the act play in the sport. In the one on-ball case listed in the chart, *Goodwin*, the accused viciously elbowed a player in the face fracturing his cheekbone, which was well outside the playing rules.

Discerning Consent

The above quote from *Brown* (1993) highlights another issue in the potential prosecution of rugby violence surrounding the legal notion of consent. Though not a sports violence case, the law of consent was thoroughly examined in *Brown* (1993), which highlighted that consent negates criminal liability where minor harm results. This creates very obvious questions and issues in the prosecution of rugby violence. These questions are succinctly queried by the UK Central Council of Physical Recreation (CCPR, 1995) as follows:

Does a player who walks on to a pitch be it cricket, football, or rugby, for example, consent to the fact that he may be injured by not to the fact that he might be seriously injured? Is it right that no one can consent to the risk of serious injury? If a rugby tackle is made within the rules of the game (i.e., not too high and not too late) but nevertheless is an extremely hard tackle, the question has to be, did the opponent consent to that tackle? Hard tackles in rugby are not only encouraged but are applauded. Any player must, we submit, therefore consent to being tackled hard by walking out onto the pitch.

There is, in effect, a consent exemption to criminal assault in the context of violent sports like rugby.

This consent exemption dates back to the 1800s, where in *Coney*[17] (1882) it was stated that, "In cases where life and limb are exposed to no serious danger in the common course of things, I think that consent is a defence to a charge of assault, even when considerable force is used" (p. 549). The question remains as to how far that exemption extends. As Omerod (2005) states, "English law's approach to the availability of a plea of consent to an offence against the person has been the subject of sustained and cogent criticism for its lack of clarity and coherence" (p. 384).

In general, consent defences can be used for common assaults but not where actual bodily harm results. In contact sports, such as boxing and rugby, actual bodily harm is commonplace and yet it is exempted from the traditional understanding and application of consent in the courts when sport is being played within the rules and in accordance with the playing culture. By stepping out on the pitch to compete, the courts assume that players are consenting to the risk of injury that is inherent in contact sports. It remains unclear as to exactly how far that consent extends, particularly for acts that are not within the playing rules.

Maintaining Public Interests

In *Attorney General's Reference* (No.6 of 1980) the Court of Appeal expressed the view that, "it is not in the public interest that people should try to cause or should cause to each other actual bodily harm for no good reason" (p. 719). In this particular case, two young men aged 17 and 18 engaged in a fist fight that led to injuries. The courts asked the question, "Where two persons fight (otherwise than in the course of sport) in a public place can it be a defence for one of those persons to a charge of assault arising out of the fight that the other consented to fight?" (p. 717). Though it was consented to, the fighting was deemed to not be in public interest. As such, the boys were not given a legal exemption from assault law.

This decision provides important guidance in two domains. First, it criminalizes street fighting that results in injury, as such fighting has been deemed to not be in the public interest. It simultaneously exempts violence that has a public interest or good. This is of particular relevance to contact sports, such as rugby, that are violent but are

---

[17] Following a bare-knuckle fighting contest, it was ruled that consent was not a valid defence to assault occasioning actual bodily harm or aiding and abetting assault for bare-knuckle fighting contests.

perceived as socially beneficial. Sports have clear benefits to both individuals and society, as organized sports,

> help maintain the citizenry's physical fitness, provide an outlet for frustrations and aggressive tendencies, satisfy the need and desire for people to prove their self-worth, provide for recreation and the pleasurable use of leisure time, and, at least with regard to team sports, train individuals to sacrifice themselves for the good of the group. (Michigan Law Review Association, 1976, p. 174)

Again, questions remain as to how far this public interest licence to violence extends, as some of the violence that occurs on the pitch is not in the public interest as it causes long-term injuries, health-care associated costs, long-term psychological harms, teaches young athletes to engage in dangerous behaviours during play, and can incite public riots and breaches of the peace.

DRAWING THE LINE: ESTABLISHING A THRESHOLD TEST FOR SPORTS VIOLENCE

Fafinski (2005) argues that, "in failing to set out clear tests to be applied in the determination of conduct sufficiently grave to be labelled as criminal, the Court of Appeal is either acknowledging that it is impossible to lay down clear guidance, or delegating the determination of criminal liability to the CPS and the jury" (p. 421). Despite the occasional intervention of the criminal courts into the sport of rugby in the UK, there remains a low degree of clarity and a general lack of guidance on when the police and prosecutors should concern themselves with violence on the pitch. As Erikson (1966) has highlighted, it is important that legal boundaries are firmly established and widely known for individuals in communities to engage in moral and appropriate behaviour. Otherwise, normlessness results, and violent and aggressive behaviours can escalate. There is a need for the establishment of a clear threshold test to determine when the courts should and will intervene into violent occurrences in sport. To consider where this threshold can and should exist, I will critically analyze the efficacy of different possible threshold tests that have been proposed and/or used.

Disciplinary Review Threshold

Establishing a high threshold for attaching criminal liability for acts of on-field violence is often perceived as favourable as internal disciplinary review mechanisms and procedures might be better suited for the task. A self-governing body in sport can ensure that punishment is swift and certain, with little doubt that the playing culture of the sport is understood. Furthermore, the punishment that a governing body can mete out can supersede that which the courts are capable of in some instances. For example, Jeffrey Standen (2008) claims that the largest penalty ever given for assault in recent United States history was the suspension given to professional basketball player

Latrell Sprewell after he choked his coach. Sprewell lost over $25 million as a result of the suspension.

Holding a similar view, the appeal judge in *Barnes*[18] (2004, para 5) stated, "The starting point is the fact that most organised sports have their own disciplinary procedures for enforcing their particular rules and standards of conduct" and later "As a result, in the majority of situations there is not only no need for criminal proceedings, it is undesirable that there should be any criminal proceedings." In contrast, in *Bowyer* (2002), it was stated that "the criminal law doesn't cease to operate once you cross the touchline of a sports field… neither does being disciplined by an employer or a sport governing body make an athlete immune to the law" (para 74). As such, legal precedent does not support a strict disciplinary review threshold, as much as many legal scholars and sport administrators might wish it did.

It can also be argued that self-governance leads to special treatment and the concealing of truth in matters of sports violence (see *McSorley*, 2000). Internal disciplinary reviews also lead to inconsistencies between sports and playing levels that seem unfair. It is more likely that professional sports will have elaborate disciplinary mechanisms and governance models in place, while amateur levels will not. As such, professional athletes are granted special leniencies that amateur athletes are not. This is a backwards approach—the harm caused by violence in professional sport is often more significant as it can cause an athlete the loss of his or her livelihood via injury, and can improperly teach young spectators to play the game dangerously.

Self-governance should be permitted within reason. The on-field contact that I have previously labeled "immoderate violence" is particularly well suited to being handled through governing bodies of sport. That said, such governing bodies should: a) be present at all levels of different sports, b) enforce penalties when necessary, and c) should be formed somewhat independently from the owners and managers who have a vested interest in profits that creates a conflict of interest in their handling of disciplinary matters at the professional levels. Overall, better, more transparent self-governance is needed. However, whether or not a disciplinary body exists and is doing their task should not be the threshold for determining if sports violence should be prosecuted or not.

Gravity of the Injury Threshold

A significant question left after the *Barnes* (2004) ruling is to what extent harm and injury resulting from on-field violence can pass the threshold of criminality. It was stated (para 5) that, "A criminal prosecution should be reserved for those situations in where the conduct is sufficiently grave to be properly categorised as criminal." Injury alone does not seem to be a determining threshold for criminality, nor should it be. In *Bradshaw* (1878), a case involving acquittal on charges of manslaughter, it was stated, "If a man is playing according to the rules and practice of the game and not going beyond it, it may be reasonable to infer that he is not actuated by any malicious

---

[18] Barnes, an amateur football/soccer player, inflicted a serious leg injury on an opposing player while making a slide tackle.

motive or intention, and that he is not acting in a manner which he knows will likely to be productive of death or injury" (para 84). In contrast, in a Canadian rugby case, *R. v. CC* (2009), the defendant was convicted of manslaughter after driving an opposing player headfirst into the ground causing fatal injuries. In this case, a degree of recklessness could be shown that driving someone headfirst into the ground would cause serious injuries and that such an act would likely cause grave injuries.

Injury alone, without recklessness and violation of playing culture, should not be sufficient grounds for crossing the threshold of criminality. For example, in the professional sport of baseball, players using a wooden bat hit a ball that is moving at over 90mph. Due to limited control of how the ball leaves the bat after impact, the ball can go straight back at the pitcher who has thrown the ball, potentially striking them in the head causing serious brain injury. Surely, the batter should not be held criminally responsible for such an injury. In contrast, if he charged the pitcher and struck him in the head with the bat directly causing a brain injury, then criminal liability should be attached.

Legitimate Sport Threshold

Voicu (2005) suggests that any behaviour that extends beyond the rules of the game should be open to criminal or civil liability. Alone, without other threshold criteria, this is a problematic stance. There are the formal rules that are often laid out in a clear fashion in the rulebook of a given sport; there are also informal rules that govern any given sport. For example, in basketball the rules state that a foul has been committed when a player on defence strikes a player on offence while the offensive player is in the act of shooting. This is the formal rule. The informal rule, or playing culture, is that if a player fouls another in the act of shooting, the foul should be hard enough to prevent the player from getting the shot up, thus avoiding a potential three-point play. Suggesting that this aspect of the playing culture of the sport should be considered criminal neglects an understanding of the sport.

A rule-based threshold could actually serve to make contact sports more risky. If violations of the rules leave athletes open to criminal prosecution, then the logical move for those in governing positions of sport, would be to make the rules less restrictive so that violent acts are not clear violations of the rules. Likewise, there would be less incentive to develop new rules that provide a safer playing environment. As Gardiner (2007) contends, "It follows that if these rules are more restrictive, but are part of the guidelines for legal intervention, there is a real danger the intervention of the criminal law will be deeper and more intrusive" (p. 24).

Barnes (2004) draws reference to a notion of "legitimate sport." Though it remains largely undefined, the accepted meaning appears to be the playing culture or the larger rules and customs governing a sport. It is my view that playing culture should be a significant consideration in determining the threshold of criminality. According to Pendlebury (2006), a problem with playing culture criteria is that they are difficult to determine. Likewise, Proctor (2012) suggests the problem with a playing culture test is the boundaries are not clear and a judge would need to have played the sport or been a significant fan to understand the culture. My perspective is that playing cultures are not overly difficult to understand, and can be understood through basic qualitative studies of different sports. Furthermore, any confusion could be clarified with players' testimony on the playing culture of their sport. As illustration, my qualitative research on Canadian gridiron football involving interviews with 59 players has revealed that clear and obvious shared understandings exist in relation to how much violence is perceived as part of their playing culture (Fogel, 2013). While rugby is a different sport than Canadian football, it is likely that similar qualitative research on players' experiences and perceptions would reveal shared understandings of playing culture and the limits of consensual violence.

CPS Threshold

Possibly the most comprehensive and detailed threshold test for prosecutorial discretion for sports violence has been developed by the Crown Prosecution Service (CPS; in Gardiner, 2007). Their list of criteria is as follows:

1. What was nature of the conduct in the context of the sport under consideration?
2. What was the degree of pre-meditation?
3. Did the offender seek to ensure that match officials were unsighted when the offence was committed?
4. Who was the conduct directed at, e.g. other participants, match officials, spectators?
5. What was the impact on those other people and their subsequent behaviour, e.g. did the incident lead to further violence or disorder on the field of play or by spectators?
6. Were there any previous incidents of a similar nature?
7. What actions have been taken by the match officials or the governing bodies in relation to the incident?

While these questions may inform context, they appear to do little in establishing a clear threshold. It is unclear how these questions would need to be answered for a prosecution to commence.

This approach is similar to that stated in *Barnes* (2004), which borrows from the *Cey*[19] (1989) criteria established in a Canadian ice hockey case, which states, "The type of sport, the level at which it is played, the nature of the act, the degree of forced used, the extent of the risk of injury, the state of mind of the defendant are all likely to be relevant in determining whether the defendant's actions go beyond the threshold" (para 15). Again, a threshold is not established. These lists of considerations are really questions without clear answers or definitive guidance provided.

---

[19] Amateur Canadian hockey player, Roger Cey, was acquitted of assault causing bodily harm after he crosschecked an opposing player in the neck.

Conclusion

For a threshold to be useful, it must be clear, rooted in an empirical understanding of playing cultures, and should balance the need to allow for sports, like rugby, to be played as they were intended but in the safest and most just ways possible. A straightforward and effective threshold test would criminalise rugby violence in cases where conduct is 1) outside the safety rules and playing culture of the sport, 2) committed recklessly or with intent, and 3) where serious long-term bodily harm results. All three criteria should be met before the criminal courts intervene. The major challenge that is posed by such an approach is that the playing cultures, and what is deemed to be reckless behaviour in a given sport, are not widely known by legal officials. However, ignorance of particular specialised fields is commonplace in legal proceedings, and there are simple, existing approaches to deal with this, e.g. expert testimony by sport researchers, referees, and current and former players.

Few sports combine the speed, person-on-person collisions, and minimal protective equipment that are featured in the sport of rugby. Established norms and rules are in place to ensure a measure of safety on the pitch; however, excessive violence continues to plague the sport leading to serious long-term injuries and the occasional death on the pitch. There is no single solution that will remedy the problem of excessive on-field violence in rugby.

Strict reliance on the criminal courts is not a viable solution, as it is not in the public interest or good for the courts to be filled with cases of on-field violence, as this would burden the courts and undermine the integrity and sustainability of many sports, especially a sport with significant body contact like rugby. Likewise, it is not in the public interest or good to allow sport to exist in a state of exemption from criminal law whereby playing sport becomes a "licence for thuggery" and incidents of sport-related serious injuries and deaths begin to rise (from *Lloyd*, 1989). A balance must be struck, with the establishment of a clear threshold test. A straightforward and effective threshold test would criminalise rugby violence in cases where conduct is outside the safety rules and playing culture of the sport, committed recklessly or with intent, where serious long-term bodily harm results. Such an approach is consistent with existing case law precedents.

CHAPTER 6

Million-Dollar Amateurs: NCAA Sport, Student-Athlete Image Rights, and Anti-Trust Law

> *Interviewee*: They can't be paid.
> *Interviewer*: Why?
> *Interviewee*: Because they're amateurs.
> *Interviewer*: What makes them amateurs?
> *Interviewee*: Well, they can't be paid.
> *Interviewer*: Why not?
> *Interviewee*: Because they're amateurs.
> *Interviewer*: Who decided they are amateurs?
> *Interviewee*: We did.
> *Interviewer*: Why?
> *Interviewee*: Because we don't pay them.[20]

The National Collegiate Athletics Associate (NCAA) has long had policies on amateurism that forbid collegiate athletes from accepting any form of compensation in relation to their persona as amateur athletes. Collegiate athletes caught violating these policies are dealt punishments, typically in the form of suspensions from play. For example, University of Georgia running back Todd Gurley was suspended for four games in 2014 and was required to serve 40 hours of community service after he accepted $3000 to sign autographs during the off-season (Staples, 2014). While NCAA sport, and NCAA football in particular, is a multi-billion dollar business, all profits generated go to the universities, the NCAA, and private enterprises. As amateurs, whose financial value can be tremendous, collegiate athletes in elite levels of collegiate sport in the United States receive scholarships and are prohibited from accepting additional payments. The legality of these restrictions have and continue to be challenged in courts of law.

This chapter examines the commercial enterprise of elite NCAA sport, with a particular focus on college football and basketball in the United States. It is argued in this chapter that this commercial enterprise is exploitative of amateur athletes who generate revenue in the millions for their universities without receiving comparable compensation or even a quality education in return. The legal issues that arise from this exploitative relationship are explored, looking specifically at the cases of *O'Bannon* (2010/2014), *Hart* (2013), and *Keller* (2010) who originally filed separate lawsuits alleging antitrust and right of publicity violations. The chapter concludes

---

[20] Transcript from an interview between former NCAA President Myles Brand and *Sports Illustrated* columnist Michael Rosenberg, 2011.

with recommendations on how the NCAA can best address the issue in a fair and lawful way, that are in the commercial interests of the NCAA, and academic and financial interests of current and former student-athletes.

THE NCAA COMMERCIAL ENTERPRISE

The NCAA and most American university administrations claim to be non-profit organizations. This claim is, however, increasingly hard to make, as NCAA revenue continues to skyrocket. In 2014, the University of Texas generated revenue of over $120 million on its Longhorns football team alone, despite a dismal 5–7 win/loss record (Smith, 2015). The NCAA has recently signed a television deal worth nearly $11 billion for television rights to the annual NCAA postseason basketball tournament commonly referred to as March Madness ("Time Warner," 2010).

NCAA coaches receive significant salaries in the major sports of football and basketball. The head football coach at the University of Alabama, Nick Saban, makes a $7 million/year salary (Edelman, 2014). In June 2014, head coach of the University of Kentucky basketball team, John Calipari, signed a $52 million contract extension; Duke University men's basketball coach, Mike Kryzyzewski, earned a reported $9.7 million in a single season (Uthman, 2014). These salaries do not take into account other potential income generated from their coaching positions in the form of corporate sponsorships, speaking engagements, coaching clinics, etc. The highest paid public employee in forty states in the U.S. is a university football or basketball coach (Edelman, 2014). Between 2012 and 2013, NCAA President, Mark Emmert, received a raise to his yearly salary from $1.2 million to $1.7 million (Westerholm, 2014). Taken together, these numbers suggest that there is tremendous revenue being generated in NCAA sport. It is clear that the NCAA is a large, and growing, commercial enterprise.

A study on the net worth of college athletes reveals that the average value of a player in a top-25 ranked NCAA basketball program in 2015 was $487,617 (Jasthi, 2015). To calculate the figure, the revenue of the top-25 ranked NCAA basketball programs was divided by 50 percent, using a mock revenue sharing model that mirrors that of the National Basketball Association. The revenue-share was then distributed among the men's basketball players on the teams, leading to an overall figure of $487,617 per athlete. When calculated on a team-by-team basis using the same formula, the top teams' players are worth over $1 million each per season (Jasthi, 2015). NCAA basketball players are million-dollar amateurs that generate huge revenues and receive only scholarships as compensation.

NCAA AND POST-SECONDARY EDUCATION

Under the grant-in-aid scholarship program at Division I NCAA schools, which is the top level of university sport in the United States, athletes are eligible to receive scholarship awards that cover their tuition, room-and-board, and course textbooks. The National College Players Association has argued that the compensation that college athletes receive places the majority of them well below the poverty line, and that the average player still pays over $3000/year in education-related expenses (Huma and Staurowsky, 2012). In the context of these impoverished conditions, it is perhaps not surprising that athletes take other forms of payment, like Todd Gurley accepting $3000 to sign autographs.

The impoverished collegiate athlete argument has not gained much public traction or support in the United States, as education costs continue to soar. In 2013 student loan debt in the United States surpassed $1.2 trillion, with the average student loan borrower $26,600 in debt (Denhart, 2013). NCAA athletes are incurring less student debt than average. They are, however, generating billions of dollars for the universities, which are offering them scholarships in ways that the vast majority of non-athletes are not. And, there scholarships are precarious: "If a revenue-producing athlete does not perform as well as expected athletically or is permanently injured, his coach can choose not to renew the scholarship without consideration of the athlete's academic performance or future" (Huma and Staurowsky, 2012, p. 7).

Furthermore, the quality of education that NCAA athletes are receiving is highly questionable. According to Huma and Staurowsky (2012) only 55 percent of NCAA football players and 48 percent of basketball players complete their university degrees. Their academic schedules are determined largely by their athletic schedules. Skipping a team meeting or practice to attend class could be grounds for revoking a scholarship. And, competition schedules require NCAA athletes to travel the country throughout the school year. According to a report at Duke University,

> We no longer determine at what time we will play our games, because they are scheduled by TV executives. This is particularly troubling for basketball, which may be required to play weeknight games away from home at 9:00pm. The potential impact on academic work is obvious, as students are required to board a flight at 2:00a.m., arriving back at their dorms at 4:00 or 5:00 a.m., and then are expected to go to class, study, and otherwise act as if it were a normal school-day. In return for large television contracts, we have surrendered control over a function that can profoundly influence the experience of our students. (Duke University, 2008, p. 11).

Providing a quality education for NCAA athletes does not appear to be the highest priority of university administrations. This is also evidenced by reports at the University of North Carolina that have revealed a corrupt academic system where athletes were steered towards taking fake classes to maintain their academic eligibility for NCAA competition (Smith and Willingham, 2015). It appears obvious that corporate, profit-driven interests continue to take precedence over the academic interests of student-athletes.

AMATEURISM VS. PROFESSIONALISM IN SPORT

There is a basic difference between professional and amateur athletes: professionals are paid while amateurs are not. In the mega-business world of elite national and international sport, the notion of the amateur athlete is disappearing, or at the very least becoming blurred. In the 1800s, distinctions were drawn between amateurs and professionals along class lines (Holt, 1992). The wealthy aristocratic elite were amateurs who did not need to work, who participated in sports as a pastime. In contrast, sporting professionals were of the working class, and professional sport held less prestige and was certainly not a lucrative occupation. Factory and other working class industrial workers would play football and rugby matches as a part-time occupation, playing for a small wage (Kemper, 2009). While some open competitions existed between amateurs and professionals, the two groups were largely separate.

In the early to mid-1900s, professional sport continued to gain popularity in spectatorship, bringing with it an influx of money allowing some athletes to be true professionals in their sport, working full-time as athletes for a particular team (Kemper, 2009). Amateur elite sports organizations remained, such as the Olympic Games, which gradually became professionalized over time (Stenk, 1988). In 1982, the IOC met to address the question of amateurism vs. professionalism in Olympic sport. By a vote of 367 to 16, a decision was reached that Olympic athletes could be paid (Downes & Mackay, 1996). Likewise, the multi-million pound business that is Rugby Union, which had traditionally defined itself as amateur sport, declared itself professional in 1995 ("Shamateurism," 1995). In the realm of multi-billion dollar elite sport, the vast majority of previously amateur leagues and organizations have defined themselves as professional, where athletes can are paid a wage for their work. In contrast, however, the NCAA has continued to maintain its claim of amateurism.

LEGAL CHALLENGES TO NCAA AMATEURISM POLICIES

Article 2.9 of the NCAA Division I Manual (2013) describes "amateurism" as follows:

> Student athletes shall be amateurs in an intercollegiate sport, and their participation should be motivated primarily by education and by the physical, mental and social benefits to be derived. Student participation in intercollegiate athletics is an avocation, and student-athletes should be protected from exploitation by professional and commercial enterprise.

Despite the multi-billion dollar commercial enterprise that the NCAA has become, and the corporate interests that steer the NCAA, e.g. game scheduling determined by TV networks, the NCAA continues to hold the stance that its athletes are amateurs participating in university sport as a recreational activity.

In order for student-athletes to compete in the NCAA, they must agree to retain their amateur status, accepting no pay or anything of value for the use of their image, likeness, or athletic talents. Furthermore, they must sign over their image rights to be used by their universities and the NCAA for an indeterminate period of time. The NCAA "protects" student-athletes from "exploitation by professional and commercial enterprises," by requiring athletes to sign their publicity rights over to the exclusive right of the NCAA for the universities and NCAA governing body to obtain and manage generated revenue.

In 2009, former UCLA basketball player, Ed O'Bannon brought forward a legal challenge to the NCAA's use of student-athlete images for profit and their failure to provide compensation to the publicized athletes. Several years after his basketball career at UCLA ended, O'Bannon noticed that the NCAA, and other third parties, continued to profit off of his image and athletic accomplishments by using his image on the front cover of a video game created by Electronic Arts (EA) Sports. Despite these profits being made, and that O'Bannon was no longer an amateur student-athlete, none of the profits were shared with him. Joined by 24 other former student-athletes, O'Bannon filed a lawsuit against the NCAA, Collegiate Licensing Company (CLC), and EA for antitrust violations and right of publicity claims under the Sherman Act (*O'Bannon v. NCAA*, 2010). The Sherman Act is a federal statute that prohibits business activities that are anti-competitive.

Samuel Keller, a former NCAA football player, launched his own lawsuit against the NCAA, CLC, and EA Sports around the same time as the O'Bannon group filed theirs, focusing specifically on a right of publicity claim from his image appearing in a video game (*Keller v. Electronic Arts Inc.*, 2010). Unlike O'Bannon, Keller sought compensation for the use of his image. O'Bannon, in contrast, sought an injunction on anti-trust grounds to force the NCAA to eliminate the rule that prohibits student-athletes from being paid for their image rights and sought compensation for the use of his image. The federal court for the Northern District of California consolidated the two cases into one (titled *In re NCAA Student-Athlete Name & Likeness Litigation*).

Former Rutgers University quarterback, Ryan Hart, filed a similar suit in a New Jersey court (*Hart v. EA Sports, 2013*). EA Sports argued that they had not violated his right of publicity, as they had creatively transformed the athletes into electronic characters that did not include their identification. The electronic athletes did, however, have the same height, weight, and visual characteristics of the NCAA athletes that played for the same teams and in the same baseball stadiums. The first court ruled that EA Sports had indeed transformed the players into their own creative expression, and that Hart was therefore unable to successfully show a violation to his publicity rights. However, on appeal, the ruling was reversed on that grounds that "[t]he digital Ryan Hart does what the actual Ryan Hart did while at Rutgers: he plays college football, in digital recreations of college football stadiums, filled with all the trappings of a college football game. This is not transformative" (para. 166). After the ruling, Hart dropped his suit to join O'Bannon and Keller in the larger class action suit.

In 2013, O'Bannon and Keller, agreed to a $40 million settlement agreement with EA and CLC, on behalf of all athletes in the class action suit, due to improperly using the likeness of athletes (Farrey, 2014). The $40 million is to be distributed to current and former NCAA players whose likenesses have appeared in EA video games, with each player receiving an estimated $4,000. The NCAA has declined any attempt to intervene in the players receiving the approximate $4,000, even though it does violate their own rules that no NCAA athlete should receive financial compensation for the use of their likeness.

The settlement left the NCAA as the only remaining defendant in the O'Bannon and Keller class action suit. The presiding judge decided that the two cases were sufficiently distinct and deconsolidated them, leaving *O'Bannon* (2014) to focus on the issue of alleged anti-trust violation, and *Keller* (2010) to center on NCAA athletes image rights. Keller quickly settled the right to publicity case in June 2014 for $20 million, which is an additional supplement to the $40 million the group of players already settled for with EA and CRC (Heitner, 2014). As such, through the settlement, the NCAA directly compensated active NCAA athletes for the use of their likenesses, going against their own by-laws.

In the *O'Bannon* (2014) ruling, the judge affirmed that the NCAA's amateurism rules do, in fact, violate federal anti-trust law, by stating,

> The Court finds that the challenged NCAA rules unreasonably restrain trade in the market for certain educational and athletic opportunities offered by NCAA Division I schools. The pro-competitive justifications that the NCAA offers do not justify this restraint and could be achieved through less restrictive means (p. 7).

Despite this, the court limited the extent of O'Bannon's victory. In *O'Bannon* (2014), the plaintiffs made three primary suggestions for less restrictive means:

(1) raise the grant-in-aid limit to allow schools to award stipends, derived from specified sources of licensing revenue, to student athletes;
(2) allow schools to deposit a share of licensing revenue into a trust fund for student-athletes which could be paid after the student-athletes graduate or leave school for other reasons; or
(3) permit student-athletes to receive limited compensation for third-party endorsements approved by their schools (p. 16).

The judge ruled that the NCAA should allow scholarships that cover all educational expenses, which would help to reduce the significant financial hardship on NCAA student-athletes. She also recommended that student-athlete publicity revenue should be awarded to student-athletes in the form of a trust fund, which would be capped at $5,000 per athlete and could be accessed after the end of a university playing career to cover additional educational expenses. The judge made no recommendation for direct compensation for the student-athletes.

The ruling did not require NCAA schools to increase their scholarship amounts or force them to create a trust fund; the judge made recommendations that would grant NCAA universities the possibility of doing so. Furthermore, on appeal, the NCAA successfully argued that the $5000 recommended trust fund for athletes was arbitrary, and that they should be scrapped. As such, despite court affirmation that the NCAA is in violation of federal anti-trust law, the key result is that NCAA schools can choose to provide a small amount of extra scholarship money to student-athletes. At the time of this writing, both O'Bannon and the NCAA have filed an appeal to the United States Supreme Court, as neither side is satisfied with the existing ruling (Berkowitz, 2016).

Conclusion

Division I NCAA sport is big business. Billions of dollars in commercial dollars flow through the NCAA enterprise each year. Despite this, the athletes who are central to the generation of this capital are living under the poverty line and receiving a low quality of education. As recent court challenges reveal, the NCAA's exploitation of student-athletes is ripe for legal controversies and challenge. Significant changes should be implemented to create fairer and more lawful policies on compensation that college athletes can receive.

Olympic athletes, who have long been held to being amateurs, are now able to pursue commercial opportunities, receiving endorsement deals, financial compensation for autographs and public appearances, and directly benefitting from the use of their persona and likeness in advertisements and merchandise. The NCAA should move towards a similar model that does not restrict athletes from accessing and realizing their potential in the commercial free market. To an extent, players are already doing so, which is then accompanied by fines and suspensions that are counter-productive to corporate interests of the NCAA, and cast collegiate sport in a negative light in the United States. It should not be a scandal for a star college football running back to accept $3,000 to sign autographs to help cover the costs of a second rate education.

It can be argued that allowing college athletes to pursue commercial opportunities on the free market will give a significant recruiting advantage to large market programs, as the top players will seek to play in locations where public exposure is highest. The result, arguably, would be an uneven playing field where small-market teams would struggle to compete. These inequities among universities already exist in their market potential, sports infrastructure, and resourcing. This argument is, however, negligible in light of the fact that these inequities lead to perennial programs that dominate their competition and others that struggle to win games.

Maintaining economic regulations that invite legal challenges from highly profitable student-athletes also continues to harm the revenue that the NCAA could be generating. For example, following the string of lawsuits, EA Sports decided to stop producing video games featuring college sports, which had previously produced revenues of over $100 million annually, with each Division I university receiving close to $100,000 per year from EA Sports (Solomon, 2013). In an uncertain legal climate, companies appear hesitant to invest in college sports despite the obvious revenue-generating potential.

The NCAA should also be doing more from within to more fairly compensate athletes for the profits that their labour helps to generate. This should start with improved measures to ensure that athletes receive a high standard of education, where academics are truly set as a priority. There are currently restrictions on the number of hours that NCAA athletes can be required to participate in competitions and practices, but more can be done to understand and take into account voluntary training hours of athletes, and to ensure that scheduling of events is in the interests of helping athletes achieve academic success, e.g. in Canadian men's university basketball games are played on non-school nights (Fridays and Saturdays), with minimal travel apart from the final year-end tournament of the top eight teams across the entire nation.

The scholarships that NCAA athletes receive should also keep them above the poverty line, at the very least covering their education-related expenses. Their scholarships should also continue past the point that their eligibility to compete as NCAA athletes ends to ensure that they are able to complete their universities degrees. Access to scholarship funds and medical benefits should not be contingent on athletic performance or participation eligibility once a NCAA athlete has competed for a university, as long as they remain academically eligible to continue at the university. If nothing else, NCAA athletes who generate millions of dollars in revenue for their universities should be well-educated amateurs who graduate with the potential to significantly contribute to the labour force in the fields of their choosing.

CHAPTER 7

Illegal Muscle: Legal Issues in Doping Control

INTRODUCTION

At the 1988 Summer Olympics in Seoul, Korea Canadian sprinter Ben Johnson shattered the 100m world record by finishing the race in 9.79 seconds. The day after his victory, urine sample tests revealed evidence of a banned steroid called stanozolol in his system. Despite Johnson's original denials of steroid use and claims of apparent sabotage, the International Olympic Committee (IOC) revoked Johnson's Olympic gold medal and world record. This was not the first time Olympic athletes had tested positive for steroid use. In the 1976 Summer Olympics in Montreal, eight of 275 tested athletes were found to have used steroids (Todd & Todd, 2001). Johnson's failed test was, however, the first to generate worldwide outrage and concern for the infiltration of drugs in sport, which continues to this day.

In this chapter, the history of doping in sport is explored by examining its genesis and development, the emergence of control policies and procedures to prevent doping, and legal challenges to doping policies and procedures. This history reveals the overall ineffectiveness of the IOC's efforts to prevent and control doping in sport. Critical attention is given to the various problems of doping control policies and procedures, such as high costs, ineffective tests, procedural errors, privacy violations, infringement on economic freedoms, and failures to consider culpability, particularly in instances of inadvertent drug use without performance-enhancing benefits, e.g. marijuana use. Serious doubts can be raised about the fairness and effectiveness of current doping control policies and strategies. It is argued that an effective strategy for the prevention of doping in sport should rest on harm reduction principles of educating athletes about the potential harms of drug use, teaching safe alternatives to achieving their athletic goals to reduce demand, and targeting traffickers of prohibited substances rather than restricting the rights and freedoms of athletes with ineffective results.

Only a small sampling of important cases over the last 30 years are discussed in this paper. The aim of this chapter is not to provide a detailed history of the development of case law on doping in sport, but rather to show the vulnerabilities of doping control policies and procedures to legal challenge. In most legal challenges, the athlete falls short in bringing forth a successful case to have their doping violation nullified. It does, however, remain troubling that continued resources are poured into maintaining ineffective, reactive doping control policies and procedures. Furthermore, claims of violations of individual rights by sports organizations and doping control officers are commonplace, which should raise concerns that doping control policies and procedures have gone too far.

THE ORIGINS AND DEVELOPMENT OF DOPING

The term "doping" is commonly believed to have originated from the root word *dop* from the Kaffir dialect of South Africa. The term *dop* refers to the use of a highly stimulating drink used by members of a tribe during religious rituals. Some accounts also suggest that Zulu warriors drank *dop* to enhance their prowess in battle. In the 1800s, Dutch settlers in South Africa adopted the term and began applying it in the context of sport. The term spread back to Amsterdam where swimmers were accused of *dop*-ing (Dimeo, 2007).

The meaning of the word doping has expanded over time. Common definitions of doping tend to resonate with the origins of the word, which involves the ingestion of a chemical substance for performance-enhancing benefits. The World Anti-Doping Code (2008, p. 8–12) has built upon this definition and defines doping as any of the following:

  i. Presence of a banned substance or its metabolites in the athlete's body.
  ii. Use or attempted use of a prohibited substance or method.
  iii. Refusing or evading sample collection.
  iv. Failure to provide whereabouts during out-of-competition testing,
  v. Tampering or attempting to tamper with any part of doping control
  vi. Possession of prohibited substances or methods.
  vii. Trafficking and prohibited substance or method.

As such, doping can now refer to a number of activities and methods beyond the ingestion of chemical substances.

It is believed that doping has a history as long as the history of sport and competition. Ancient Greek athletes supposedly ate the testicles of lambs believing it would provide special strength in sports such as wrestling, boxing, and running. Likewise, Roman gladiators are said to have used stimulants from plants that were believed to improve endurance and courage making them fiercer in competition (Mottram, 2011).

Early accounts of doping in modern sport, beginning in the 1800s, indicate the use of various stimulating chemicals and drugs such as heroin, cocaine, caffeine, and amphetamines, particularly within bicycle racing (Yesalis & Bahrke, 2002). In the 1904 Olympics, the coach of United States marathon runner Thomas Hicks admitted that the runner had used strychnine and brandy during the race to fuel his performance, which was not prohibited at the time. In a 1955 bicycle race, five of 25 riders tested positive for amphetamine use. Following several amphetamine-related deaths, including British cyclist Tommy Simpson, the use of amphetamines in sport began to be considered a serious issue in the 1960s (Todd & Todd, 2001).

The most significant development in doping has been the discovery of the positive effects of anabolic steroids on muscle growth and recovery. Early scientific research on anabolic steroids revealed that, "it changed them, and fundamentally... after many months on testosterone, their chest and shoulder muscles grew much heavier and stronger... it caused the human body to build the very stuff of its own life" (de Kruif, 1945, p. 226). Steroids offered athletes more long-term gain than other performance-enhancers, as there were greater long-term benefits for muscle gain, as compared to the short bursts of energy from amphetamine stimulus. After its discovery, and before the advent of reliable testing in the mid-1970s, steroid use was widespread in sport. A poll of track and field contestants at the 1972 Munich Olympics found that 68 percent were using anabolic steroids (Todd, 2001).

The mid-1970s and onwards can best be described as a science or "bio-medical war in sport," in which new designer substances are continually manufactured, alongside new masking agents, while doping control agents and scientists have struggled to keep up (Fogel, 2013, p. 283). On occasion, high profile cases like that of Ben Johnson, the East German Olympic team, Lance Armstrong, or of countless Major League Baseball players give the suggestion that dopers will be caught. Most doping, however, continues to go undetected. It is estimated that "the probability of detecting a cheater who uses doping methods every week is only 2.9 percent per test" (Hermann & Henneberg, 2013, p. 2).

DOPING CONTROL POLICIES AND PROCEDURES

Alongside the development of different drugs and doping techniques, various policies and governing bodies have been inaugurated in a failed attempt to prevent the widespread use of drugs in sport. This section will now turn to overviewing the key points and developments in the history of doping control policies and procedures.

The first major stand against doping in sport was taken by the International Association of Athletics Federation (IAAF), the governing body for the sport of track and field, in 1928 (Gleaves & Llewellyn, 2014). The IAAF outlawed the use of stimulating substances. Many international federations followed their lead, but doping control measures were limited to policy and ineffective, as reliable tests had not yet been developed.

Following the death of British cyclist Tommy Simpson in 1966, the International Olympic Committee (IOC) established a medical commission to fight doping. Drug tests were first introduced at the Olympic Winter Games in Grenoble and at the Summer Games in Mexico in 1968. The tests were, however, expensive, limited in the number of substances they could detect, and riddled with problems that lead to false positives and false negatives (Mottram, 2011). According to a former United States Olympic team drug tester, "The athletes knew better than anyone that the drug testing posed little threat to them. They scoffed at the testing notices and went right on with their routine drug use with little fear of detection" (Voy & Deeter, 1991, p. 79). Although it was widely known that anabolic steroids were being used at this time, testing methods for steroids were insufficiently developed and did not allow for their inclusion on the banned substances list (Mottram, 2005).

Anabolic steroids were not added to the IOC's list of banned substances until 1976, as reliable tests were not developed until 1974. The 1976 Summer Olympics in Montreal were the first Olympics with testing for anabolic steroids and eight of 275 tested athletes were found to have used steroids (Todd & Todd, 2001). It was not until Ben's Johnson's failed drug test in the 1988 Olympics, after he had won the 100m gold medal, when a moral panic took hold based on the notion of a drug-epidemic sweeping sports (Taylor, 1991).

By the beginning of the 1980s, an apparent increase in the number of international sports-related, many of which doping-related, disputes led to the IOC creating and funding an independent, international tribunal for sports disputes. In 1984, the independent tribunal was established called the Court of Arbitration for Sport (CAS). CAS has since become a significant authority in the resolution of doping related disputes.

The next major initiative of the IOC in relation to doping was to convene the First World Conference on Doping in Sport in Lausanne in 1999. Major problems plagued doping control in international sport, and the goal of the conference was to strategize on solutions. Some of the problems that needed to be addressed included: a lack of consistency and compatibility of doping rules in different sports, lack of consistency of testing and policies in different countries and federations, high costs of doping control measures, legal challenges of test reliability, and difficulties with out-of-country testing (Houlihan, 1999).

It was decided that the solution to these problems would be to develop unified standards and coordinated efforts of sports organizations and public authorities. Following the proposal of the Conference, the World Anti-Doping Agency (WADA) was established. Following the Copenhagen Declaration on Anti-Doping in 2003, WADA unveiled its *Code* to be used as a guide and authority for governing bodies of sport to develop harmonized anti-doping policies aimed at protecting athlete's health, preserving fair play, and fostering the spirit of sport. By 2004, in large part due to IOC requirements for participation in the Summer Olympics in Athens, most sports organizations adopted the WADA code (Hunt, 2011). Athletes are bound to anti-doping policies of WADA, and their national sport governing body developed thereof, via a contractual relationship by participating in the sport.

LEGAL CHALLENGES TO DOPING CONTROL POLICIES AND PROCEDURES

Testing procedures for doping are largely ineffective (Fogel, 2013). Historically, athletes have been shown to beat doping tests through: (a) corrupt pay-offs to doping control officers, (b) playing the odds, relying on the low likelihood of ever being tested in many sports (e.g. in Canadian football, less than 10 percent of players are tested in a given year), (c) timed drug cycling, by strategically using drugs at times when they are least likely to be tested, (d) low dosages, since the tests allow for some individual variance in naturally produced substances (termed endogenous production), (e) masking agents, which cover up the use of banned substances, (f) cleansers, which rid the body of traces of drug use faster, (g) urine replacement, and (h) using newly designed substances that tests do not exist for yet (Fogel, 2013). While some of these approaches have become less effective with the development of new drug testing approaches and technologies, it remains highly unlikely that doping athletes are ever caught.

When athletes have been successfully caught for doping violations, it has given rise to countless challenges in legal and arbitration courts, requiring further resources in the continued losing battle against sports doping. Historically, common areas of challenge, with mixed success, have been on the grounds of: i) procedural issues, ii) culpability, and iii) economic freedom. The future of legal challenges of the policies and procedures for doping will likely be on the grounds of privacy rights, religious rights, and other human rights violations (Valkenburg et al., 2014). The very establishment of CAS in 1984 was, by in large, a function of the need to deal with doping-related challenges and to ensure that the controversies remained within the realm of sports governance (Gardiner et al., 2006).

Procedural Issues

As part of the disciplinary proceedings for doping infractions, sports governing bodies must show that the procedures for collecting, storing, and analyzing testing samples were carried out correctly. Challenges of unreliable tests, chain of custody violations, unfair hearings, and lack of establishing burden of proof have been frequent.

In the case of *Modahl* (2001), testing samples went unrefrigerated in hot Lisbon temperatures for two days before they were tested. Also, the chain of custody documents in the case were missing for the athlete's "A" test. When her "B" sample was opened there was a strong ammonia odour and a pH of 9 (normal is 5). Despite these issues, doping control officers tested it anyways and both samples showed significant levels of testosterone in her body. She received a four-year suspension. On appeal, Diane Modahl was able to successfully show that the conditions under which the samples were stored could have led to bacteria formation, which could cause a failed testosterone test. Modahl then brought a challenge against the British Athletics Association (BAF)[21] on the grounds that she was denied a fair hearing, another procedural issue, though she was unsuccessful in that particular claim.

In *Varis* (2008), a suspension was overturned despite a positive test for erythropoietin (EPO) after procedural errors were made. In this instance, WADA provisions granting the right to be represented at the opening and analysis of the B sample was violated. As a result, the B sample was rendered invalid leading CAS to cancel the sanction imposed on her by the International Biathlon Union (IBU). The case reveals that anti-doping authorities and laboratories do not always follow their own rules, and that the consequence of this can be an overturned decision.

In *Reynolds* (1994), United States track and field athlete and Olympic gold medalist, Butch Reynolds, appealed a suspension after a positive test for nandrolone on the grounds of an undermined testing process. He successfully argued that the doping control room was not secured or guarded while the doping control officer had left his control station, which undermined the validity of the procedures and results. The argument that his sample could have been switched or sabotaged was deemed possible by the courts and his suspension was eventually overturned. Reynolds was later awarded $27,356,008 following an action against the IAAF on the grounds of: breach of contract, breach of contractual due process, defamation, and tortious interference with business relations.

---

[21] Which is now UK Athletics.

Culpability

Possibly the most controversial aspect of the World Anti-Doping Code (WADC) is the adherence to the legal concept of strict liability. The WADC affirms that:

> For purposes of anti-doping violations involving the presence of a Prohibited Substance (or its Metabolites or Markers), the Code adopts the rule of strict liability... Under the strict liability principle, an anti-doping rule violation occurs whenever a Prohibited Substance is found in an Athlete's bodily Specimen. The violation occurs whether or not the Athlete intentionally or unintentionally used a Prohibited Substance or was negligent or otherwise at fault (Article 2.1.1).

Intent, therefore, is not considered an element of determining guilt in a doping offense. If a prohibited substance is found in an athlete's body, an anti-doping violation has occurred. Despite regular protest that this violates principles of natural justice, both CAS and the English High Court have held that a strict liability rule is lawful as it might be the only way to effectively police doping.

The position of the courts to allow the continued use of strict liability principles by WADA and national sport organizations was firmly entrenched in *Quigley* (1994).[22] In the case it was stated:

> It appears to be a laudable policy objective not to repair an accidental unfairness to an individual by creating an intentional unfairness to the whole body of other competitors. This is what would happen if banned performance-enhancing substances were tolerated when absorbed inadvertently. Moreover, it is likely that even intentional abuse would in many cases escape sanction for lack of proof of guilty intent. And it is certain that a requirement of intent would invite costly litigation that may well cripple federations—particularly those run on modest budgets—in their fight against doping. (p. 129)

The statement argues that fairness to an athlete is of lesser concern than ensuring that a drug-enhanced athlete, regardless of how they got that way, does not compete in sport.

In *Baxter v. IOC* (2002), the British alpine skier Alain Baxter was stripped of his bronze medal won at the 2002 Winter Olympics in Salt Lake City for inadvertent use. Baxter, who had a documented history of nasal congestion issues, had ingested an over-the-counter medication containing the banned substance levometamphetamine. He regularly used the same product in England without issue, but had purchased the medication in Salt Lake City unaware that the product had a different formulation in the United States. Although the panel found that that Baxter did not intend to ingest

---

[22] Quigley, a competitive shooter, fought a ban following a failed drug test caused by his use of a medicine for treatment of bronchitis, which he was suffering from.

the substance, he was nevertheless found guilty of the doping offense and his disqualification was upheld.

In *Gasquet* (2009), a tennis player appealed a suspension from the International Tennis Federation (ITF) for cocaine use on the grounds of no fault or negligence. Richard Gasquet argued that he had not used cocaine and that trace amounts of cocaine in his body were the result of kissing a young woman who had used cocaine, without his knowledge of her use. The ITF tribunal accepted the argument, and imposed a lesser suspension of two and a half months rather than the WADA prescribed sanction of one year. WADA exercised its right of appeal to CAS, but same result was decided upon.

In a similar case, a Brazilian athlete tested positive for traces of an anabolic steroid called clostebol. He claimed that he was contaminated as a result of sexual intercourse with a woman who had administered a medication containing clostebol for a vaginal infection. Despite scientific proof than an athlete could test positive after sexual intercourse with a woman using this medication, the athlete was held strictly liable (Pereira et al., 2004).

In most of these and other similar cases, the substance the athlete has tested positive for through inadvertent use is not even a definitive performance-enhancing substance. According to article 4.3.3 of the WADA Code, for a substance to be prohibited, it must meet two out of three of the following criteria:

1. Medical or scientific evidence of performance enhancement
2. Medical or scientific evidence of potential health risk
3. WADA determination that substance or method violates the spirit of sport

The spirit of sport provision remains highly vague and controversial; it can even be argued that the spirit of sport—to win and compete at the highest levels possible—encourages and normalized the use of performance-enhancing substances (Ritchie, 2012). Given that spirit of sport remains a vague, unclear concept any substance regardless of its performance-enhancing benefits can end up on the prohibited list. And, the WADA code states in clear terms that the prohibited list is final and, as such, challenges to the list are not permitted. The result is that you can have unsuspecting athletes banned from their livelihood for trivial, accidental violations that have little or no effect on performance-enhancement in sport. Banning athletes on these grounds seems contrary to the spirit of sport rather than promoting it, and will continue to result in legal challenges.

Economic Freedom

It has been shown by the courts that there are inherent economic aspects of sport. Therefore, sport cannot have a complete exemption from treatises of economic rights and EU competition law. Article 6 of the UN Covenant on Economic Rights states that: "The States Parties to the present Covenant recognize the right to work, which includes the right of everyone to the opportunity to gain his living by work which he freely chooses or accepts, and will take appropriate steps to safeguard this right."

Likewise, Article 1 of the European Social Charter states the requirement to: "protect the right of the worker to earn his living in an occupation freely entered upon." EU competition law is the most straightforward example of economic regulation that has an impact on sport. Article 81 of the Treaty Establishing the European Community (1995) states:

1. The following shall be prohibited as incompatible with the common market: all agreements between undertakings, decisions by associations of undertakings and concerted practices which may affect trade between Member States and which have as their object or effect the prevention, restriction or distortion of competition within the common market.
2. Any agreements or decisions prohibited pursuant to this Article shall be automatically void.

Banning athletes from competition and therefore, in many cases their livelihood, just because they used substances that are often not illegal to possess or use could be seen as a violation of economic freedom rights.

In *Meca-Medina* (2006), this was one aspect of their legal challenge. In the case, two swimmers were banned for four years following positive tests for a prohibited substance. The two swimmers aimed to prove that anti-doping rules were in breach of EU competition law as it restricted their economic freedom to pursue their careers. While their appeals were largely unsuccessful, the case does raise questions about the fairness of current anti-doping strategies. On the one hand the performance of an athlete is a commercial commodity to be bought and sold, while on the other, they are disqualified for getting caught using performance-enhancing drugs to help them improve their performance and commercial value thereof.

Conclusion

From the ancient Greeks eating lamb testicles to Lance Armstrong using EPO, doping in sports competitions has had a long history. The future possibilities for engaging in doping are vast, particularly with much theoretical discussion of the potential for gene doping in sport (Miah, 2004; Naam, 2005). WADA's response to the doping threat in sport has been to wage what Alexander (2014) has termed a "war on doping in sports" (p.1). Even in rare cases where athletes who are using prohibited drugs test positive, the highest likelihood is that it is for marijuana, which has been shown to not have performance-enhancing benefits in sport yet remains on the WADA prohibited list. Serious doubts can be raised about the fairness and effectiveness of current doping control policies and strategies.

If doping control is seen as a competition between drug testers, drug designers, and athletes, then designers and athletes appear to have a sizable advantage and are winning the competition. The testers are restricted by budgetary constraints, limited testing technologies, and the need to keep up with ever changing pharmaceutical advances. A reactive approach on the part of doping control officials does not and cannot work effectively, yet WADA's approaches are primarily reactive. An effective strategy for the prevention of doping in sport should, instead, rest on harm reduction principles of educating athletes about the potential harms of drug use, teaching safe alternatives to achieving their athletic goals to reduce demand, and targeting traffickers of prohibited substances rather than restricting the rights and freedoms of athletes with ineffective results.

CHAPTER 8

Pay-to-Play: Online Fantasy Sports, Gambling, and the Law

INTRODUCTION

To address the unique legal issues created by the widespread emergence of Internet gambling, the United States Congress enacted the Unlawful Internet Gambling Enforcement Act (UIGEA) in 2006. With a threat of criminal sanction, the UIGEA prohibits internet-based businesses from accepting money transfers from financial institutions in the United States for the purpose of unlawful online gambling. The UIGEA does not restrict all online gambling activity, and fantasy sports are among the forms of online gambling that Congress did not seek to criminalize. While the UIGEA does not criminalize fantasy sports at the federal level, state laws have not been as definitive. The actual legality of online fantasy sports in the United States remains unclear.

This chapter focuses on exploring the legal aspects of online fantasy sports as a potential form of gambling and looks specifically at gambling laws and legislation in the United States. Many other forms of law are relevant to online fantasy sports, such as patent law, copyright law, and trademark law; however, those other forms of law are beyond the scope of this chapter. This chapter explores the extent to which gambling laws have been and should be applied to online fantasy sports.

WHAT ARE FANTASY SPORTS?

Fantasy sports are contests between participants, who act as team managers and compete in leagues with fictional teams comprised of real athletes. Participants select the athletes typically through a draft and free agent system, which mimics real professional sports leagues. Fantasy sports are now managed almost exclusively through online systems. While it is common for fantasy sports to be free for participants, some fantasy sports charge participants an entry fee and offer them a chance to win additional money through a fantasy league championship.

The statistics the real athletes accumulate in their sport are awarded to the fictional team in the fantasy league. If it is a basic rotisserie format, the fantasy team in the league with the best overall accumulation of real player statistics at the end of the season is the winner. If it is a basic head-to-head format, fantasy players/teams compete against a single fantasy team each week and typically win or lose based on the statistics their players accumulate in that week; fantasy teams in a head-to-head league are then ranked by number of wins.

In recent years, daily fantasy sports competitions have become more popular, particularly in a pay-to-play format (Steinberg, 2014). The significant difference of daily fantasy leagues over traditional season-long fantasy leagues is that the competitions typically last for a single twenty-four-hour period. Daily fantasy sports leagues are organized in many ways, but the most common is through a salary cap system with an open league that has a guaranteed prize for the winner. The salary cap system mirrors actual professional sports teams, whereby fantasy owners are allotted a set salary amount that they can spend on assembling a team of players, who are each assigned a value to select. Unlike a season-long league where only one owner can own a particular player, in a daily salary-cap competition, many owners can own a same player. The salary cap system introduces a new level of analysis for the participant, as they must assess the actual value of a player compared to their assigned value and likely statistical output. Participants then construct their teams by spending within the salary cap, competing against thousands of others who have done the same, with the chance to finish first and win a set prize, e.g. $10,000. Although the speed at which daily fantasy competitions occur has raised additional concerns of legality, the format and structure is not that much different from season-long fantasy sports to create different or unique challenges.

There are many variations of fantasy sports procedures, both with season-long and daily leagues, but the basic concept is comparable among different sports, leagues, and fantasy sports providers. Fantasy sports participants conduct research on and estimate the likely statistical performances of real athletes to create fantasy teams that win or lose based on the statistics their players achieve in real life. Fantasy sports are games of statistical analysis and prediction.

THE FANTASY SPORTS INDUSTRY

In 2012, over 33 million Americans participated in fantasy sports competitions (Subramanian, 2013). While many of the participants play in free fantasy leagues, of those who pay entry fees, an accumulated total of $1.44 billion was paid in the United States towards league registration. Further to this, Subramanian (2013) estimates that fantasy players spend over $1.6 billion on fantasy sports-related purchases, such as online services, draft kits, magazines, and enhanced sports television programming. As such, fantasy sports have quickly become a multi-billion dollar industry in the United States.

The tremendous popularity of fantasy sports competitions has coincided technological advances of computer programs and the Internet, which provide simple tools to operate fantasy sports, such as calculating and compiling advanced statistics. Furthermore, the Internet allows for fast sharing of information and removed geographic barriers to participation. Early fantasy sports leagues would have relied on paper, pencils, calculators, and league-reported statistics; online sports statistics now appear online in real-time and online fantasy sports providers have systems that automatically compile statistics, results, and standings. The Internet has also become a major source of fantasy sports news and advice, where advanced fantasy sports analytic programs can be purchased, and advice on the best players to add/drop can be sought on fantasy sports websites, blogs, and podcasts.

Gambling Laws and Online Fantasy Sports

There are many statutes that prohibit certain forms of gambling in the United States such as the *Professional and Amateur Sports Protection Act* and *Illegal Gambling Business Act*. Neither specifically address fantasy sports competitions, nor have been used to bring forward challenges to the legality of fantasy sports competitions. In 2006, the United States Congress enacted the Unlawful Internet Gambling Enforcement Act (UIGEA), which did specifically address online fantasy sports by providing an exemption to the new laws as long as the fantasy sports competitions are also run in a manner that is consistent with state gambling laws.

Section 5362(E)(ix) of the UIGEA exempts fantasy sports on the condition that: i) the winning prize is established in advance of the competition and are not determined by the number of participants, ii) winning corresponds to the knowledge and skill of participants and are determined by the statistical results of athletes in real sports competitions, and iii) no winning outcome is determined by a score, point-spread, or other performance-indicator of a single sports team or athlete.

The condition most open for debate is the requirement that winning correspond to knowledge and skills of participants. In fantasy sports there is, undeniably, a significant element of chance as results are not predetermined and can be influenced by factors that are difficult to predict such as injuries to athletes, weather conditions, players suspensions, etc. The distinction between skill and chance is not a dichotomous one. It is a matter of predominance. That is, does the activity require a greater degree of skill or chance to determine a winning outcome? As the judge in *Turner*[23] (1995) stated, "the character of a game is not whether it contains an element of chance or an element of skill, but which is the dominating element that determines the result of the game."

The predominance test—or dominating element test—does not, however, immediately resolve whether fantasy sports are legal under state gambling laws as it is not immediately clear if fantasy sports are based more on skill or chance, and not all states have a clear predominance test. Furthermore, the UIGEA does not supersede state gambling laws, which leaves open the possibility of legal challenges under state laws. The Tenth Amendment authorizes states to regulate gambling. Gambling-related activities are regulated in all fifty states as well as the District of Columbia.

State Challenges

In 2006, attorney Charles Humphrey filed a lawsuit in New Jersey against many fantasy sports providers including Viacom Inc., the CBS Corporation, the CBS Television Network, Sportsline.com, Inc., the Hearst Corporation, the Walt Disney Company, ESPN, Inc., Vulcan Sports Media, and The Sporting News. In his complaint, Humphrey argued that the fantasy sports websites were in violation of gambling laws in the District of Columbia, Georgia, Illinois, Kentucky, Massachusetts,

---

[23] The defendant, Bruce Turner, was arrested and charged with gambling offences for operating a street sidewalk game that encouraged pedestrians passing by to place bets on whether they could determine under which cap an item could be found.

New Jersey, Ohio, and South Carolina, and that all losses suffered by fantasy sports participants should be recovered.

Humphrey argued that fantasy sports leagues are a form of illegal gambling as participants wager a fee for the chance to win prizes, and that winning prizes in fantasy sports is significantly based on chance. The court rejected Humphrey's argument that the fee was a wager, ruling instead that it was a one-time payment for an online service being rendered. If competition entry fees where prizes are awarded were interpreted as a wager, many competitions could be deemed to be gambling, e.g. a youth basketball team that pays a $300 tournament entry fee with the chance to win tracksuits for finishing first in the tournament. If, for example, the tournament prize money changed based on the amount of money a team submitted before the tournament, the teams predetermined odds of winning, and the number of other teams that entered, it could then be seen as a wager. However, if the nature of the prize is unconditional and a standard fee is paid to play, the courts do not deem it to be a wager, as evidenced in the *Humphrey* decision.

The *Humphrey* (2006) case was dismissed without detailed discussion of skill versus chance or the predominance test in fantasy sports. Although the court effectively reaffirmed the UIGEA's legalization of fantasy sports, it did not answer the persistent question of whether fantasy sports are games of chance or skill under the predominance test used by most states to determine the legality of contests under state gambling laws.

Another case, *Langone v. Kaiser and FanDuel* (2012), was the first challenge to daily fantasy sports competitions in a court of law. The case was, however, dismissed on the grounds that the complainant, Christopher Langone, did not have appropriate grounds for filing the lawsuit as he did not fit the definition of "loser" in the Loss Recovery Act of Illinois. The court went further to state that even if Langone had qualified as a "loser," that the fantasy sports provider, FanDuel, would not qualify as a "winner" because they received their payment through commission, and the amount they earn is not determined by the outcome of a particular sporting event. As with *Humphrey* (2006), the court did not address whether daily fantasy sports are games of skill or chance.

No court has explicitly examined online fantasy sports competitions with the predominance or dominant element test. However, a Washington Supreme Court did rule that football pools are chance-dominated as "weather, the physical condition of the players and the psychological attitude of the players" are integral to the outcome of sports competitions (see *Seattle Times v. Tielsch*, 1972). There are chance elements in fantasy sports, but there is a higher degree of skill required than in picking winning teams in pool competitions. Chance occurrences can also be controlled for more in fantasy sports competitions where, for example, an injured player can be dropped from a team in exchange for a player on the free agent list on the day of a game. In contrast, decisions in pools are typically made by a deadline and then are locked in for the duration of a season or playoffs. The likelihood that a fantasy sports participant could draft players without a familiarity with the real league that the fantasy league is based on and with minimal understanding or research on player statistics and be successful is very small.

While there is an element of chance involved, fantasy sports are games of statistical knowledge, research, prediction, and skill. While the predominance test has not fully played out in a courtroom, it appears likely that fantasy sports would be understood as games predominantly determined by skill. As such, this provides a significant legal protection. Some states do not, however, rely on a predominance test. For example, Arkansas, Iowa, and Tennessee rely on an "Any Chance" test (Ehrman, 2015). Given that there is a definite element of chance in fantasy sports, legal challenge is especially possible in these states. Likewise, under Montana law, it is legal to participate in fantasy sporting contests unless a wager is made over the Internet or telephone. Other states, including Kansas and Arizona, have written statements on their state gaming websites that denounce fantasy sports as potentially illegal activity when the host collects a percentage of entry fees (Ehrman, 2015). The uncertainties of how state gambling laws could be applied in these and other jurisdictions has prompted many fantasy sports providers to restrict access to paid entry competitions in several states.

WHY SHOULD MOST FANTASY SPORTS BE EXEMPT FROM GAMBLING LAWS?

Gambling is widely considered to be a serious social and psychological issue that has the potential to cause significant financial hardship, motivate economic and property crimes, and contribute to substance abuse issues (Dixon et al., 2006). Gambling laws have been created to place regulations and restrictions on gambling to minimize potential harms. Fantasy sports gambling can be argued to pose less of a threat of harm, and therefore criminalizing them would be unneeded and could potentially create added risks and harms, as will be outlined in this section.

In terms of financial hardship, entrance fees for fantasy sports competitions are fixed in advance, and are either nominal or free. For an individual to accumulate a significant debt, they would need to register a high number of teams competing simultaneously. Given the time commitments necessary to compete successfully in fantasy sports, it is unlikely that anyone would seek to manage more than a few teams at once. Furthermore, sports seasons can take several months before a potential winning prize is awarded, further adding to the unlikelihood of excessive financial investment in fantasy sports by a single participant (Thompson, 2001). Daily fantasy leagues can lead to heightened spending in short periods of time and as such, should receive closer scrutiny and regulations.

A central concern related to sports gambling is the potential for the integrity of sporting competitions to be compromised through game-fixing, point-shaving, bribes, and the involvement of organized crime in amateur and professional sports (Hill, 2010). In fantasy sports, there are minimal integrity issues that arise, because players, coaches, and referees are unlikely to alter their individual performance to influence fantasy sports results. No individual player, team, or game has determining significance on the outcome of a fantasy sports competition. The combinations and permutations of fantasy team compositions make it infinitely complex for athletes and referees to alter their performance to rig fantasy sports contests.

It could be argued that fantasy sports are a slippery slope into the world of sports gambling and might therefore have a corrupting influence on young participants. That is, people might start by playing fantasy sports and then over time move towards other illegal means of sports gambling that they otherwise would not have pursued. However, Thompson (2001) argues that the corrupting influences are negligible, and are really no higher than a child buying a pack of baseball cards. For a pack of baseball cards a young fan will pay a few dollars for the chance that the pack might contain a valuable card or one that will eventually become valuable. Buying baseball cards is not considered to be gambling, or a slippery slope towards sports gambling, or a corrupting influence on children. Purchasing cards, as with playing fantasy sports, is a fun activity that raises interest and knowledge about sports and athletes for young fans.

It could also be argued that fantasy sports actually have a deterrent effect on illegal forms of sports gambling. Research has shown that wagering money on sporting contests increases the level of interest of sport viewers, adding a new level of excitement to sport viewership (European Gaming & Betting Association, 2015). Fantasy sports competitions provide a legal, regulated way for sports viewers to enhance their engagement with sports without involving themselves in illegal sports gambling enterprises. Profits generated are then taxable rather than sustaining organized criminal activities and enterprises.

Criminalizing fantasy sports would have a significant economic impact. As previously discussed, fantasy sports are a multi-billion dollar industry in the United States. Protecting their financial interests, the NFL and MLB sent representatives to congress to lobby for a fantasy sports exemption from gambling laws. According to Cabot and Csoka (2007), professional sports organizations in the United States had two primary interests in ensuring the legalization of fantasy sports:

> The first was preserving increasing revenues. The future of fantasy sports would have been placed in jeopardy if Congress passed internet gaming legislation that could have been read to prohibit fantasy sports. The second was maintaining increased viewership by individuals who played fantasy sports (p. 8).

Allowing and regulating fantasy sports permits a highly profitable and taxable industry to continue to grow and flourish.

There are also social benefits to fantasy sports competitions. Fantasy sports games are often played by groups of friends, in the privacy of their own homes, for fun without any of the participants making a profit. Friends gather to draft fantasy teams, discuss trades of players on their teams, and debate the fantasy values of real players. Online forums allow for further discussion among people across different geographic regions who share a common interest in a particular sport or sports. Fantasy sports are very much a social activity. Strict legal restrictions on fantasy sports would undermine a positive social activity for millions of participants.

Conclusion

Online fantasy sports are a multi-billion dollar industry in the United States, and yet the laws pertaining to the industry remain somewhat unclear and undecided. In *Humphrey* (2006) and *Langone* (2012), the respective courts ruled that fantasy sports do not constitute illegal gambling, which is consistent with the Unlawful Internet Gambling Enforcement Act that was passed by United States Congress in 2006. Differences in state gambling laws have, however, kept some uncertainty over the legality of fantasy sports in some states, such as Arizona, Iowa, Louisiana, and Montana where fantasy sports providers have restricted participant access to pay-for-play fantasy competitions.

Unusual formats for fantasy sports that stray from the traditional skill-to-chance ratios should be examined on a case-by-case basis to determine legality. Gambling laws should not apply to fantasy sports that are based on standard season-long and daily leagues, where set entry fees are paid, winning outcomes are determined by the performance of multiple real-life players, the winning prize or prizes are predetermined, and where knowledge and skill are clearly required to compete successfully.

CHAPTER 9

Sports in the Courts and the Rise of Alternative Dispute Resolution: A Critical Analysis of Sport Dispute Resolution Mechanisms

INTRODUCTION

In *McInnes v. Onslow-Fane* (1978),[24] the presiding judge stated that sports bodies themselves are "far better fitted to judge than the courts." Traditionally, courts do not intervene in the vast majority of sports conflicts and disputes, with some notable exceptions such as violations of criminal law, cases of restraint of trade, and breaches of the rules of natural justice (Gardiner et al., 2006). While sports clubs and organizations can typically remedy most disputes internally through negotiation or internal review panels, occasionally this is not the case. Rather than head straight to the courts for dispute resolution, which can be flawed even in select circumstances when a judge is willing to hear a case, many sports governing bodies are turning to alternative dispute resolution (ADR) mechanisms, such as mediation and arbitration. This chapter highlights the potential shortcomings of sports litigation and offers a critical assessment of the suitability of using ADR in its place.

SPORTS IN THE COURTS

Conflict and disputes in sport, as with any social institution, are commonplace. Turner (1996) highlights this point by stating "there is more law to be found in today's newspapers in the sporting columns than on any other pages" (p.14). Likewise, Haslip (2001) states "conflict in sport is inevitable, regardless of how well the sporting enterprise is conducted" (p. 248). The increased commercialization of sport beginning in the 1970s, including significant corporate sponsorship of amateur sport after the 1984 Los Angeles Olympics that have been dubbed the "Hamburger Olympics" (La Rocco, 2004, p.12), has given rise to more frequent disputes and conflicts. The commercialization of sport has heightened the financial implications of sport, and accordingly, the legal implications (McLaren, 1998). As Blackshaw (2008) states, "Now that sport is big business nationally and internationally, it is not surprising sports disputes—especially commercial ones—are on the increase" (p. 1). This increase in sport disputes increasing became an increase in sports litigation.

The reliance on the courts to remedy disputes in sports has some significant limitations. First and foremost, court processes tend to be slow and subject to delays, and can take months if not years to be settled. Sporting disputes are often of an urgent

---

[24] A boxing manager filed a court appeal after his was refused a manager's licence by a boxing association.

nature. The case of *Garrett v. Canadian Weightlifting Federation* (1990) provides a good example. Garrett was a member of the Canadian National Weightlifting team and was set to compete in the 1990 Commonwealth Games in New Zealand. Months before the competition, Garrett was notified that he was being replaced on the team by an inferior weightlifter who he had beat in previous competitions and who happened to be a member of the local club of the national team coach. In response, Garrett filed a court order seeking reinstatement of his spot on the national team.

The judge agreed that he should rightfully be on the team, and that he had been replaced on the basis of personal bias of the coach. However, the team roster had already been submitted for competition, and the court order was not binding to the international organization, so it was too late for Garrett to compete in the Commonwealth Games. The courts are simply too slow to handle many legal disputes in sport. Beyond the delays caused by slow court processes, there is also an issue that some of the norms and intricacies of sport might not be adequately understood and accounted for in a court of law. For example, if weightlifter A, who beat weightlifter B in preliminary competition, was replaced by weightlifter B for an upcoming competition, there might be a compelling sporting reason for doing so that could be overlooked in a court of law. It could be that neither weightlifter had a reasonable chance at earning a medal in the competition, but weightlifter B was younger, less trained, and had more potential to earn a medal in a later competition than weightlifter A. An inflexible court judge who does not understand and appreciate certain norms of sporting competition might see weightlifter A as more deserving of a spot on the team simply because he won a preliminary competition. That might, however, have a detrimental impact on the long-term success of the team.

Court proceedings are also costly. Legal fees paid by all parties involved in a dispute that goes to court can easily exceed £35,000 per dispute, even if a dispute involves a financial dispute that is valued at nowhere near that amount (Slaikeu & Hasson, 1998). These costs can also be prohibitive for many individuals seeking fairness and justice in sports because they might not have the finances to bring forward a lawsuit, nor would they want to risk the possibility of paying additional legal fees if they were to lose the suit. As such, the use of courts to solve disputes in court can be costly, inefficient, and prohibitive of seeking justice.

Another issue is that most courts of law are adversarial in structure and orientation. For the resolution of some conflicts this is not overly problematic, as the parties might not have close working relationships that will need to continue after the conflict is remedied. As McLaren (1998) identifies, the institution of sport is characterized by community, cooperation, teamwork, and close working relationships. Adversarial approaches to dispute resolution can damage relationships, threaten teamwork, and heighten conflict between parties who must continue working together. As such, an adversarial approach to dispute resolution in sport is not appropriate in many cases, especially commercial disputes, and might in fact heighten some conflicts rather than resolve them.

Historically, courts have been reluctant to interfere in conflict and disputes in the realm of sports. According to McArdle (2015), "the courts were famously—and usually quite properly—loathe to intercede in sports' bodies determinations" (p. i).

This is not always the case, but generally speaking there is a notion that there are "some kinds of dispute which are much better decided by non-lawyers or people who have special knowledge of or expertise in the matters giving rise to the dispute than a lawyer is likely to have" (Healy, 2009, p. 28). This is increasingly the case with the rise of alternative dispute mechanisms in sport, as the courts can direct or recommend mediation, arbitration, or other non-adversarial forms of dispute resolution. As such, for the most part the courts are not serving as a willing mechanism in the resolution of conflicts and disputes in sport.

Overall, the use of courts to remedy conflicts and disputes in sport has be fraught with problematic issues including: i) slow and delayed decisions, ii) jurisdictional issues, iii) lack of specified knowledge surrounding the intricacies and norms of different sporting contexts, iv) high costs that are often disproportionate to the monetary value of the dispute, v) adversarial in process and orientation leading to a breakdown in cooperative sporting relationships, and vi) a general reluctance of the courts to delve into disputes in sport. Generally speaking, courts are not a particularly suitable arena for the resolution of many disputes that arise in sport, particularly for disputes related to disciplinary authority, eligibility rules, team selection, financial entitlement, commercial agreements, and doping infractions. By contrast, cases involving potential federal or national law violation, e.g. manslaughter on the field, should remain the domain of national courts. These shortcomings, as well as heightened demand for dispute resolution that has coincided the commercialization and corporatization of sport, has led to a rise in the use of ADR in sport. The result has moved sports further away from the courts.

ALTERNATIVES TO THE COURTS

ADR rests on the notion that "people should first try to solve their own problems, if necessary seek the assistance of a neutral third person, or call on the community that is affected by the problem to reach a solution that satisfies everyone" (Yates et al., 2000, p.129). ADR involves dispute resolution outside of a court of law. According to Epstein (2013) "the most important aspect of ADR, as opposed to litigation, is that final agreements or decisions are not made by judges" (p. 407). There are countless ADR variations, although each can typically fall into the category of i) negotiation, ii) mediation, iii) arbitration, or a combination thereof (Yates et al., 2000). These categories can also be seen as steps in an increasingly structured and binding approach to resolving disputes. In what follows, the benefits and limitations of each approach will be assessed looking specifically at the topic of contract and revenue disputes in sport for comparisons purposes.

Negotiation

Typically, the first option in resolving a dispute is through negotiation, which is characterized by direct communication between disputing parties to reach an agreement (Corbett, 2003). Generally speaking, negotiation entails an informal format, no facilitator in the resolution process, and the goal of achieving consensus on a resolution that both parties are amenable to. According to Baker and Esherick (2013), "this method of resolving disputes is no more difficult than making a phone call or sending a letter offering to sit down and discuss the issues" (p. 124). That might be somewhat of an overstatement of the simplicity of negotiation, but it has the potential to work that well just as it can also not work in some cases.

There are clear and obvious benefits to solving disputes through negotiation. First of all, it can save considerable costs and fees in comparison to court litigation, mediation, and arbitration (Goldberg et al., 1992; Moore, 1997). In fact, it does not need to cost anything if parties represent themselves in the negotiation. It also has the potential to lead to quick decision-making, which can be essential in the context of sport as the previously discussed *Garrett* (1990) case highlights. Negotiation can also help to foster cooperation and teamwork and build capacity for problem-solving within sports organizations allowing them to be better equipped to remedy possible future disputes. It is also a flexible approach that can be shaped to the needs of the parties involved in the dispute. It can also allow for confidential decision-making, keeping a dispute from reaching the tabloids and other mass media, which can potentially damage the goodwill of one or more of the parties involved in the dispute.

Resolving disputes through negotiations can also have several limitations and challenges (Goldberg et al., 1992). First of all, most sporting disputes are between individuals and groups who hold different amounts of power and influence. As such, negotiations are not likely to occur on equal footing. This can result in an unfair agreement that significantly benefits one party over the other. Unfair agreements reached through unfair negotiation are then susceptible to legal challenge, erasing any benefits of a negotiation-based approach. Negotiation also requires voluntary participation, which might not be achievable in some disputes. Likewise, personal issues and emotions of disputing parties might interfere with being able identify issues and interests, and develop agreeable solutions. Negotiation can also be used as a stalling technique, to delay potential proceedings or in an attempt to exhaust filing deadlines. Lastly, sometimes negotiation just does not work because both sides are unwilling to compromise in a dispute, e.g. the National Football League (NFL) lockout in 2011, National Basketball Association (NBA) lockout in 2011, National Hockey League (NHL) lockouts in 2005 and 2012, Major League of Baseball (MLB) strike in 1994, etc. When negotiations break down, other forms of dispute resolution become necessary either through the courts or further ADR mechanisms.

Mediation

In mediation, a mediator meets with all parties to a dispute, explores the issues of the dispute, encourages collective problem solving, and often makes recommendations on resolving the dispute. The recommendations of a mediator are not legally binding for the parties involved in the dispute (Corbett, Findlay, & Lech, 2008). When the National Basketball Players Association (NBPA) and NBA were unable to reach a consensus on the terms of a new collective agreement in 2011 through the use of negotiation, they entered the process of mediation (Zillgett, 2011). At that point, the NBA had locked out the players for over 100 days, putting the entire NBA season in jeopardy. While the two sides were not in agreement on many aspects of the collective agreement, the furthest gap between them was over splitting basketball related income (BRI) between the owners and players. The previous collective agreement had a BRI of 57 percent, which the NBA argued was causing the vast majority of teams to lose money and run on a deficit (Stein, 2011). The NBPA argued that the NBA was using deceptive economics, and they were unwilling to agree to lower the BRI to under 53 percent. The owners were unwilling to go over 47 percent. As a result, the players and owners reached an impasse in their negotiations. An independent arbitrator of the Federal Mediation and Conciliation Service (FMCS), George Cohen, was brought in to mediate the dispute (Zillgett, 2011). In the early stages of mediation, Cohen met separately with the owners (NBA) and the players (NBPA) to hear the interests of each side. The sides were then brought together, and reached a BRI agreement of 50 percent (plus or minus 0.65 percent per season depending on projected income), and the basketball season was saved albeit with a shortened sixty-six-game regular season rather than eighty-two games (CBA, 2011).

The resolution of the 2011 NBA Lockout provides an example of where mediation of disputes in sport can work effectively. As the example illustrates, the process of mediation involves an independent, neutral third party (mediator) helping the parties in the dispute come to a mutual agreement by facilitating negotiations between them (Blackshaw, 2002). The mediator may offer suggestions and point out overlooked issues, but he or she does not have the power to make a binding decision or award; their role is to facilitate discussions and help the disputing parties come to an amicable agreement (Corbett, Findlay, & Lech, 2008). Mediation agreements are not binding until they are in the form of a written and signed settlement agreement or contract (Blackshaw, 2008). Mediation can be entered through i) voluntary agreement of the disputing parties, ii) obligation under a contract or agreement, iii) obligation under a national law or policy, or iv) court order or encouragement in some countries (Blackshaw, 2008).

There are definite benefits to solving disputes through mediation. First of all, the process can be fast and efficient in comparison to litigation, arbitration, or stalled negotiations. The costs are also typically lower than arbitration and litigation, though there is still a cost of hiring a mediator and potential legal counsel. Mediators can offer new perspectives and ideas on negotiations, with the potential of creative solutions that satisfy both parties. The disputing parties remain in control of the process, keeping it "within the family of sport" (Blackshaw, 2008, p.1). It can also help to build capacity for problem solving between the disputing parties, which could be beneficial in future potential disputes with each other or others. Disputing parties are also more likely to be able to maintain good working relationships, which is essential to the business of sport, following a non-adversarial mediated settlement (Gardiner et al., 2006). Furthermore, negotiations and materials produced during mediation are confidential. Typically, the mediator and parties involved agree in writing to not disclose any information, without the consent of the other parties. Likewise, both parties typically agree in writing that a mediator will not be called as a witness in any possible subsequent litigation that might arise after the mediation (Epstein, 2002). This allows for protection from what Blackshaw (2008) terms "washing their dirty sports linens in public" (p. 1). The negative publicity that can surround disputes in sport, particularly those of a commercial nature where both sides could be perceived as greedy and selfish, can be avoided through mediation. Finally, and possibly most importantly, mediation often works. According to the ADR Group, who mediate over 12,000 cases per year worldwide, the success rates of mediation by their group exceed 94 percent (ADR Group, 2000).

Despite the overwhelming benefits of mediation, it is not without potential limitations. One limitation is that due to the confidential nature of the negotiations and settlement, cases cannot serve as deterrents in instances that might involve misbehaviour (Gardiner et al., 2006). The confidential nature also means that others are not able to learn from the negotiation process and avoid similar disputes or find solutions to their existing disputes. Likewise, this creates a challenge for legal scholars studying sports disputes, as there is restricted access to mediated cases for analysis and discussion, and possible subsequent recommendations for sports managers to mitigate conflicts and disputes in their organizations. There is also a potential for mediation to be used to unfairly gain information from the other party in bad faith negotiating (though information gained through mediation is intended to be confidential, and should not be permitted as evidence in a court of law).

Mediation can also not work if one or both of the disputing parties refuse to participate or are unwilling to fully participate and buy into the process (Gardiner et al., 2006). For example, in 2014, a complaint was filed by female soccer players to the Ontario Human Rights Tribunal on the grounds of sex discrimination for the planned use of artificial turf for the 2015 FIFA Women's World Cup in Canada. The Canadian Soccer Association (CSA) has ruled that artificial turf is significantly cheaper (especially in Canada where there is inhospitable weather for year-round grass), and is more durable, and equally as safe as grass. However, the female soccer players have argued that artificial turf results in more injuries and changes the style and speed of play. Its use for the Women's World Cup, they have contended, is discriminatory because it denotes differential treatment from male elite athletes in the World Cup, who have never played on artificial turf (Keogh, 2014). The Ontario Human Rights Tribunal recommended mediation in the dispute; however, the CSA refused to enter into mediated negotiations with the female soccer players. The players did not take their complaint any further, and the Women's World Cup has remained on artificial turf.

Arbitration

Arbitration involves submitting a dispute to a neutral third party (an arbitrator or arbitration panel) for a final resolution of a dispute (Epstein, 2013). Arbitration decisions are final and binding unless otherwise agreed in advance by the disputing parties. The agreement to use arbitration to settle disputes is typically found in a contract or collective agreement, although it is also possible to enter arbitration voluntarily or by court order in some circumstances and jurisdictions (Epstein, 2013). Arbitration can be similar to a court, mimicking an adversarial trial but with more relaxed rules of evidence and procedures. Given how close it can resemble a court process, as it involves an arbitrator who makes a final decision, arbitration is considered by some to not even be an alternative mechanism (ADR Group, 2000). However, the more conventional view is that arbitration is in fact a form of ADR (see Corbett, Findlay, & Lech, 2008; Epstein, 2002, 2013; Healy, 2009; McArdle, 2015; Moore, 1997; Yates et al., 2000).

The benefits of arbitration are similar to mediation. The process is confidential, private, and less formal than litigation. Arbitration can also allow for a more timely hearing through expedited processes, and is typically lower in cost than litigation (Corbett, Findlay, & Lech, 2008). It is also a more flexible process, with the potential to be conducted over the phone or in an ad hoc tribunal setup in an informal setting. Furthermore, arbitrators can be selected for their expertise in both law and particular sports; in contrast, judges in a courtroom might know little of the "culture, ethos, and practical realities of the sport domain" (Corbett, Findlay, & Lech, 2008, p. 221). The increasing use of arbitration, and other ADR mechanisms, for disputes in sports also places less demand on the legal system to remedy issues in sport.

Arbitration decisions are not open to court challenge or appeal unless the arbitrator has engaged in egregious, erroneous, or fraudulent conduct, or has significantly exceeded the boundaries of their authority. This does, however, mean that disputing parties who do not agree with an arbitrator's award will not try to appeal it in a court of law. For example, in 2004, NFL player Ricky Williams decided that he did not want to play football anymore (*Miami Dolphins v. Williams*, 2005). His team, the Miami Dolphins, filed a grievance demanding that Williams repay the $8,616,343 that he had received in bonuses and incentives. The grievance was heard by an arbitrator who granted the Dolphins' grievance. Williams, in turn, filed a motion in district court arguing that the arbitrator had overstepped his authority by violating laws and public policy of the state of Florida. The district court heard the motion, but denied it on the grounds that the arbitrator had made his decision within his authority.

Though Williams's grievance was unsuccessful, it is possible to have an arbitration decision in the context of a sports dispute vacated by a court of law. For example, in 1993 the National Football League Players Association (NFLPA) informed Washington's NFL team that 37 players had not paid their union dues and should be suspended from the team under rules of their collective agreement (*Nat. Football Lea. Players v. Pro-Football*, 1994). Washington did not comply, prompting the NFLPA to file a grievance, which prompted an expedited arbitration. The arbitrator granted the NFLPA's grievance. In turn, Washington filed a motion in district court to vacate the arbitrator's decision on the grounds that it violated Virginia law and public policy. After hearing the case, the court agreed that the arbitrator's decision was in violation of Virginia law and vacated the award.

These cases reveal a potential limitation of arbitration that it can simply be one step on the way to litigation. However, such cases are more the exception than the rule because arbitration decisions tend to be final and binding, with courts rarely giving consideration to vacating awards. The difficulties of overturning an arbitration decision could also be seen as a potential limitation, as the binding decision might not be a particularly good one and less potential for appeal exists than within the legal system (Epstein, 2013). Furthermore, the confidentiality and privacy of arbitration processes and decisions come with the issues of reducing potential deterrence and preventing researcher access. Private arbitrations also create transparency issues, which could be seen as unfair to the public who want to know the details of a sports dispute and settlement. Also, while arbitration is often termed "relatively inexpensive," it can still be quite expensive to a point where it can exceed the cost of litigation (Roberst & Palmer, 2005).

INTERNATIONAL ADR

The Court of Arbitration for Sport (CAS) has become the leader in international sports dispute resolution (Nafzinger, 2004). It has been described by some as the "Supreme Court of World Sport" (Beloff, 2012, p. 71). It is not the only international ADR mechanism used for sports disputes, but it has quickly become the primary mechanism. The CAS provides mediation, consultation, and arbitration services, though its court-like functions are associated with its role as an arbitral service. Cases typically appear before the CAS through voluntary submission or contractual obligation, e.g. all Olympic athletes must sign an agreement for any sporting disputes to be resolved by the CAS (Gardiner et al., 2006).

Mediation and arbitration services of the CAS have many significant advantages. In comparison to other mediation and arbitration services, and especially compared to litigation, there is a definite expertise in the complexities and intricacies of sport. It is also suited to handling sporting disputes that cross international borders, which many sporting disputes do, as there are nearly 300 mediators and arbitrators on the CAS from 87 countries with expertise in the laws of different jurisdictions (CAS, 2015). Their expertise in handling sporting disputes also grows as they continue to handle cases and build knowledge related to sports disputes and international laws. The CAS handles approximately 300 sports disputes cases per year (CAS, 2015). Their procedures are flexible and can be expedited, e.g. tribunals for quick arbitration decisions are setup at each Olympic games. The costs are also relatively inexpensive, and both parties receive estimated costs before the services commence (CAS, 2015). CAS services involving commercial disputes are typically confidential, while disciplinary appeals such as doping disputes are typically published unless otherwise requested by the disputing parties (CAS, 2015). The CAS has also served one of the important functions that led to its creation, which was to keep sports disputes, particularly those relating to doping, from placing undue burden on legal systems.

As with other arbitration decisions, CAS arbitrations are not open to court challenge or appeal unless the arbitrator has engaged in egregious, erroneous, or fraudulent conduct, or has significantly exceeded the boundaries of their authority. This has been seen by some as a major limitation of the CAS, which positions it as a "supreme court" that could be seen as violating principles of fundamental justice and the right to a fair trial (Cernic, 2012). The CAS does, however, have an appeal option that has yet to be widely used, for instances when the right to a fair trial may have been violated or where there is lack of jurisdiction. Judicial recourse is to the Swiss Federal Tribunal. One example where a CAS award has been vacated is *Matuzalém*

(2008, 2009, 2011, 2012). Matuzalém had breached his contract with FC Shaktar Donetsk of the Ukrainian Premier League. Due to this breach of contract, the CAS subsequently determined that Matuzalém and his new Spanish club Real Zaragoza owed Shaktar €11.9m. Matuzalém then appealed the CAS award to the Swiss Federal Tribunal (SFT), arguing that the decision was unfair and disproportionate. The SFT determined that the CAS award was lawful and upheld the decision. Matuzalém failed to pay the award, prompting Shaktar to request that FIFA's Dispute Resolution Chamber (DRC) enforce the award. The DRC gave Matuzalém and Real Zaragoza a 90-day deadline to pay the award, an additional fine, and a suspension until the award was paid in full. CAS upheld the DRC decision. Matuzalém appealed this second CAS decision to the SFT, and this time the decision was determined to be disproportionate and illogical. If he was unable to play football he would be unable to earn the money to pay Shaktar. Matuzalém and Real Zaragoza still had to pay Shaktar €11.9m, but the SFT overturned their suspension. This suggests that the CAS is not supreme, as there is a higher court that can overturn CAS decisions. According to James (2012),

> This conditional autonomy ensures that in the vast majority of cases, sport is able to regulate itself, but where the fundamental rights of parties are compromised, the courts will readily review the sporting justice system to ensure that it operates fairly (p. 65).

The Matuzalém contract dispute points to other potential limitations of the CAS. For one, it is not a guarantee that litigation will not occur. This single contract dispute went to the SFT two times following two separate CAS decisions. Furthermore, it shows that there is no guarantee of a quick decision. The Matuzalém contract dispute spanned several years. Beyond Matuzalém, CAS services are not always quick; the average CAS arbitration case takes six to twelve months for resolution (CAS, 2015). There are also potential jurisdictional issues that can arise related to CAS arbitrations, and corresponding questions of which laws should be used in rulings. In the Matuzalém case, the breach of contract occurred in Ukraine, but his contract did not specifically state which laws would apply. In such cases, the CAS reverts to Swiss Law (CAS, 2015). However, the CAS does endeavour to interpret and apply laws of different countries when they are stipulated in contracts or agreements.

The Matuzalém case is a rarity in sports law and arbitration. CAS has been widely recognized as a binding international sport arbitration system. One example of this is the case of German speed skater Claudia Pechstein, who was suspended by the International Skating Union (ISU) in 2009 after a doping test revealed "irregular blood parameters," but no definitive evidence of doping. She appealed to CAS who upheld the suspension (*Pechstein*, 2009). She then made multiple appeals in the Swiss courts without success in overturning the CAS decision. In 2014, the German Olympic Sport Association (*DOSB*) tasked an expert commission to explore the case scientifically, which found that there was no evidence of doping. Armed with more medical and scientific evidence, Pechstein filed another appeal in a German court, who affirmed the authority of CAS in ruling on the matter and dismissed her appeal (Ruiz, 2016). The authority of CAS has been further entrenched.

Conclusion

There is no panacea for conflicts and disputes in sports. The courts can be particularly flawed because of their slow and delayed decisions, jurisdictional issues, lack of specified knowledge surrounding the intricacies and norms of different sporting contexts, high costs, adversarial process and orientation leading to a breakdown in cooperative sporting relationships, and a general reluctance to delve into disputes in sport.

Negotiation, mediation, and arbitration can provide certain advantages over litigation in many cases by reducing costs, building problem-solving capacity, maintaining good working and business relationships, ensuring privacy and confidentiality, and allowing for quick and flexible processes and decisions, while ensuring that independent experts in both sport and law are aiding in dispute resolution. These approaches can also serve to complement each other in what can be termed hybrid dispute resolution, commonly used in multi-issue cases (Haslip, 2001). While at one time litigation might have been the conventional form for settling disputes in sports, the rise of ADR mechanisms and hybrid approaches have led to useful developments in the realm of sports law.

CHAPTER 10

Future Directions in Sports Law, Regulation, and Dispute Resolution

INTRODUCTION

Despite increased case law and legal scholarship on the topic of law and sport, the precise role of law in the regulation of sport remains unclear and controversial in many circumstances. This lack of clarity of the law's role in sport has given rise to the question of how to best regulate and govern sport. As sport becomes increasingly globalized and commercialized, new disputes will continue to erupt that cross international borders and incorporate laws and legal systems of different sovereign nations. Technological advancements are changing the way sports are played, viewed, and managed, which raises new ethical and legal discussions, e.g. the legality of gene doping, and other medically and technologically driven human-enhancements, in sport. Large-scale social movements, e.g. disability rights, gender identity rights, animal rights, etc., will also shape legal reform and enforcement, which in turn will create new legal clashes with sport.

Other regulatory issues in sport, such as those discussed throughout this book, will undoubtedly continue. Athletes will violently assault each other in their sports. Tremendous revenue will continue to be made in and around sport, and disputes will inevitably arise about who gets what, particularly between the athletes who perform the mental and physical labour on the field and the owners and managers who facilitate the functioning of the teams and leagues in which the athletes compete. As has become widely known and documented in recent years, players, coaches, and/or referees, will continue to facilitate profit making for organized criminal enterprises through match-fixing. Unfair and unlawful marketing of athletes and teams will not cease. Performance-enhancing drugs and masking agents, as well as other human enhancers, e.g. blood/ oxygen doping, will continue to be used leading to public controversies and national shame.

There is little doubt that many significant issues will continue to plague the management and organization of sport, at amateur and professional levels, and in countries worldwide and at international sporting events. The important question to be asked is how to best regulate sport to minimize harms, protect the integrity of sport, and maximize the benefits of being involved in sport in assorted capacities. The law alone is not an answer to the question. While the law might serve an important role in providing guidance, mechanisms, and support to solving issues in sporting matters, the courts do not have the capacities, expertise, or resources to provide a panacea.

Legal and sport scholars have proposed a number of legal and regulatory reforms to help to effectively resolve various problems and disputes that continue to arise in national and international sport. This section critically assesses seven of these legal and/or institutional reforms including: 1) increased formal social control, 2) self-regulation, 3) balanced legal reform, 4) establishing separate national laws on sport, 5) creating and expanding independent sports violence tribunals, 6) reorienting sport, and 7) furthering the development of sports law as a distinct and established legal field.

Increased Formal Social Control

The increased formal social control approach holds that the best way to deal with problems in sport is to increase the frequency and severity of formal punishment, such as court imposed fines and criminal sanctions (Gulotta, 1980; Voicu, 2005; Yates & Gillespie, 2002). The belief of those who posit an increased formal social control approach is that it serves as a deterrent that can keep athletes from engaging in deviant acts, e.g. prison sentences for athletes who commit acts of deliberate violence, and sport managers and owners from conducting exploitative, unethical, or corrupt business practices, e.g. FIFA president Sepp Blatter received an eight-year suspension—later reduced to six—from all football-related activities for making a disloyal payment, and now faces potential criminal sanction (Conn, 2015).

A drawback of the increased formal social control approach is that it is largely reactive; it is a response to deviance and corruption rather than a clear means to preventing it. There is a deterrent component, but it is primarily directed at the individual who committed the act and it might not serve the purpose of general deterrence to all athletes and administrators. For formal social control to be effective, it would require widespread publicity of the punishment, sending a warning to all athletes and sport administrators that there unlawful and/or unethical actions will have certain and severe punishments.

Another issue of an increased formal social control approach is that it has the potential to individualize problems. For example, when a Canadian ice hockey player punches an opposing player in the head causing irreversible brain damage leading to a conviction of criminal assault, criminal liability for the incident is placed squarely on the offending player who perpetrated the violent offence (see *Bertuzzi*, 2004). This is a somewhat simplistic perspective on sports violence as it fails to address and remedy the larger sports culture that the act occurred within. Additionally, it fails to understand the liability of coaches, team owners, league management officials, etc. who have potentially tolerated and promoted violence in their sport (Fogel, 2013).

Severe punishment to individual athletes in sport can also have significant and harmful repercussions to individuals who are in no way at fault in the deviant or unlawful occurrence. For example, if an athlete is convicted of criminal assault and spends time in prison, that could significantly harm the success of his team. The team might then fail to make the playoffs. Season ticket sales might decrease. The sports tourism industry in the city where the convicted player plays might lose thousands or millions of dollars in revenue. And, even after the player is released from prison, with a criminal record he could be barred from crossing international borders. In a league like the NHL where players must regularly play in both Canada and the United States, the player's career could be significantly shortened. Millions in salary and endorsements could be lost by the player, and by the sports industry around him, for a punch to an opposing player, which is a fairly regular occurrence in the sport.

An increased formal social control approach also places a greater burden on the courts and, law enforcement officials more generally, to deal with sports problems and disputes, which is a complicated and often ambiguous area of law, as has been highlighted throughout this book. Legal officials do not have the resources or expertise to take a leading role in the resolution of problems and disputes in sport. It is more reasonable for the courts to provide guidance on sporting matters, and intervene in cases that involve criminal conduct or cannot be solved through more efficient means.

Autonomous Self-Regulation

Another proposed approach to dealing with issues and disputes is to promote heightened self-regulation within sport, rather than looking to outside sources (Eugene & Gibson, 1980; Standen, 2008). The rationale behind the self-regulation argument is that the penalties that can be provided within a sports league tend to be quick and certain, and are delivered by individuals with enhanced knowledge of the rules and playing cultures within the sport. In contrast, measures taken that follow the formal social control approach are often long and drawn out as court cases can take months if not years to be resolved. Potential internal penalties can also be quite severe, beyond what a court might be able to impose, e.g. a sixty-game suspension for violating a drug policy could cost a Major League Baseball (MLB) player upwards of $10 million, which is more severe penalty than a court would likely impose.

One significant issue of a self-regulation approach is that inherent conflicts of interest can occur. For example, disciplinary decisions might be clouded by the pursuit of profits, such as a league disciplinary review committee not wanting to suspend a star hockey player for an act of excessive on-ice violence, as his absence from play could reduce ticket sales for an upcoming match. Or, a governing body of collegiate sport might create rules that ensure they reap all profits from the image, likeness, and persona of their student-athletes.

Another issue is that the governance structures of most organized sports, and their relationships with the legal systems in their jurisdictions, already allow for a high degree of self-regulation and yet problems and disputes continue to exist in sport. More self-regulation might heighten many problems in sport governance rather than resolve the issues. Those involved in the management, governance, and regulation of sport from within sports organizations should, however, work to ensure that they are creating rules and procedures that enhance the safety of the sport, are fair and beneficial to those involved in sport, and are compliant with existing laws.

Balanced Legal Reform

A third possibility to address problems and disputes in sport is through balanced legal reform. The goal of this approach is not increased formal social control, as this is perceived as being "as troublesome to apply as it is intrusive on play" (DiNicola & Mendeloff, 1983, p. 845). Nor is it to let self-rule in sport prevail. Instead, the aim is to strike a balance between the need for formal social control in sport and the importance of self-regulation. It is a middle ground between the last two approaches discussed.

Such reforms could include writing formal legal or policy provisions that provide guidance to the courts and sports organizations on when, how, and why the courts should handle particular matters versus when self-regulation should be relied upon. For example, the word "sport" is completely absent from the Criminal Code of Canada. This creates confusion surrounding if and when violence in Canadian sport can be considered criminal. A balanced legal reform approach could involve a paragraph being included in the Criminal Code that specifies the criteria for sports violence to be considered criminal violence. Sports violence that does not meet the criteria would then be the domain of self-regulation within a sports league or organization. Along these lines, White (1986) proposes that laws should be clarified through a variety of "bright-line tests" (p. 1048). The purpose of White's bright-line tests would be to set clear guidelines for determining acceptable versus non-acceptable violence in sport. For example, it could be that acts of non-consensual violence become criminally prosecutable if they exist after a play has been whistled down, while acts occurring during play are given leniency.

Such legal reforms could have positive results in that laws could be made to be much clearer as they relate to sport, increased legal attention would be paid to the intricacies of sport, and laws could be created in ways that do not over-privilege sport while ensuring sporting fairness and integrity. It would also help to clarify jurisdictional issues of what legal entity or governing body is responsible for handling which problems and disputes in the context of sport.

Establishing Separate National Laws on Sport

Rather than adding sport provisions into existing laws, another possibility could be to create a separate set of federal laws that pertain exclusively to sport. For example, in 1983 in the United States, a bill was proposed to establish federal laws concerning violence in sport, which was titled the Sports Violence Arbitration Act. The bill outlined potential penalties for excessive on-field violence, which were limited to "a fine of not more than $5,000, imprisonment for not more than a year, or both" (as cited in Underwood, 1984, p. 82). This particular U.S. bill did not pass, nor has anything similar passed since, largely because existing laws on assault and other violent transgressions are already in place and appear to be understood as adequate.

With such an approach, distinct laws and penalties pertaining to sports could be established with detailed procedures on responding to problems and disputes. Other separate national laws exist relating to areas like transportation, the environment, hazardous waste, oceans, etc. There could be national sports laws. Unlike the unsuccessful 1983 bill, these laws could be more comprehensive than focusing purely on sports violence, and could cover other issues such as: i) other potentially criminal acts, e.g. hazing rituals, match-fixing, doping, gambling, etc. ii) commercial issues, e.g. ambush sports marketing, revenue-sharing, image rights, licensing and merchandising, etc., and iii) human rights, e.g. access, discrimination, privacy, etc.

Creating new laws for sport that replace existing laws could be seen as an unfair legal exemption granted to sport or a privileging of sport. While some exemptions appear to exist in practice, new laws would formally codify such an exemption which policy makers have been reluctant to do. Likewise, exclusive sports laws could end up being more severe than existing laws, causing an unfair application of laws to athletes and sports managers. Rather than establishing separate laws for violence in sport that would exempt sport from existing laws, it seems more in keeping with the rule of law to incorporate sport into existing laws and legal processes, as was outlined in the previous section on legal reform. Any new laws pertaining exclusively to sports that are created should not replace existing laws, but should be in keeping with existing laws and perhaps serve only to provide additional clarification.

Creation and Expansion of Independent Sports Disputes Tribunals

One interesting aspect of the 1983 Sports Violence Arbitration Act is that it would have required the formation of a special court of arbitration to handle cases of on-field sports violence. As discussed in Chapter 9, similar mediation and arbitration services have been established for sports disputes, such as CAS with great success in reducing the burden on the courts, decreasing legal costs, providing timely decisions, allowing for privacy and confidentiality in proceedings, while ensuring that independent experts in both sport and law are aiding in dispute resolution (Blackshaw, 2002; Epstein, 2013; Haslip, 2001; Healy, 2009; McArdle, 2015).

The CAS and other sport-specific mediation and arbitration services have to date been somewhat limited in the sports disputes that they handle. The use of arbitration in sport is typically related to disputes over eligibility rules, team selection, financial entitlement, and doping infractions (Barnes, 1996). These services could, however, be expanded to handle more sport related problems and disputes, such as determining appropriate sanctions in incidents of on-field violence, providing guidance to remedy human rights violations, and providing third-party insight into commercial disputes in sport.

Independent sports tribunals allow for specialized knowledge of the intricacies and norms of the sports, while upholding existing law by an independent, unbiased third-party. It would also allow for swift and certain judgments. Ideally, these judgements would not be held in-camera as most arbitration hearings are, because the tribunal decisions could serve to provide both guidance on handling sports disputes and deterrence from engaging in misconduct. Given how established many existing independent arbitration services are, such as Sports Resolutions in England and the CAS internationally, this approach might not require the establishment of new tribunals. It could mean the expansion of the existing tribunals to more locations that address a wider range of sports problems and disputes.

Reorienting Sport

Most people start participating in sport for enjoyment, recreation, health, improved coordination and physical literacy, and community. The increased commercialization and corporatization of sport, even at the amateur levels, has changed the ways in which people experience sport. For example, writing on his perceptions of changes in amateur (AAU) youth basketball in the United States, Jay King (2009) states,

> Over the years, AAU basketball has evolved from an organization dedicated to providing an outlet for children to improve skills and develop valuable skills such as teamwork and leadership to an industry designed to put money into its leaders pockets. The steady evolution has left AAU basketball in the hands of sleazy, money-hungry businessmen rather than conscientious adults with the kids' best interests at heart (p. 2).

Both the NCAA and AAU provide proof that even amateur sport in the United States has become a commercial enterprise.

Many sporting disputes could potentially be prevented by reorienting sport, particularly at the amateur playing levels, away from corporatization. Policies, programming, and educational initiatives could be established that emphasize the health benefits of sport, long-term athlete development, and overall physical literacy. Restrictions could be placed on amateur sports, e.g. limited corporate sponsorship of amateur teams.

While in theory it might be seen as viable to reorient sport towards a focus on play and physical health, the reality is that sport is intricately tied to corporate interests. The Olympic movement and intense corporatization of the Olympics over the last few decades aptly illustrates this. Athletes are workers, even at amateur levels, whose labour helps to generate tremendous profits. And, as long as professional leagues are highly corporatized, the ties between sport and the commercial world will remain. Imposing restrictions on the commercial aspects of sport could also be unlawful under competition and anti-trust laws in different jurisdictions.

Furthering the Development of the Field of Sports Law

As discussed in Chapter 1, there is ongoing debate about whether or not sports law is a distinct field of law. At present, it is different than many other fields of law that rely primarily on specific legislation and particular courts. Sports law crosses over many different areas of law such as such as: criminal law, administrative law, civil law, contract law, employment law, labour law, procedural law, community law, and so forth. Sport is also governed by particular rules within sports, as well as internal disciplinary tribunals.

As this book has shown, the role of law in sport is complex. Further developing the field of sports law, in terms of both research and practice, will allow for increased specialization of legal professionals with knowledge of the intricacies of sport and the law, as well as further research in law faculties and in the social sciences on issues related to sports law. Further development to the practical and academic field of sports law will help lead to important legal and institutional reforms to alleviate serious problems and disputes in sport.

CONCLUSION

The interaction between sport and law is complicated. There is no single approach that can remedy all of the issues and disputes that are ongoing in sport. This concluding chapter has explored various possible approaches to improving the handling of sports problems and disputes. The optimal approach would be one that combines the various approaches in a balanced way, taking the strengths from each while minimizing the weaknesses.

More research, specialized training, and education should be done in the area of sports law in law and sport management programs in North America and worldwide. Clearer guidelines should be established on when and how the courts will intervene into sporting matters, versus when and how sport organizations should handle matters on their own. Sporting provisions and clarifications should be added to existing laws, or separate laws should be established that are in keeping with existing laws without unfairly privileging or impairing sport. And, finally, sport dispute tribunals should be expanded in both their scope and jurisdictional availability to provide independent arbitration with expertise in the intricacies of sport, avoiding conflicts of interest that are inherent to self-regulation, providing efficient, expedited service, and ensuring that laws are applied to sport fairly and in accordance with the principles of natural justice.

REFERENCES

Abrahamson, A. (February 11, 2006). Lund is barred from Games: The U.S. skeleton racer says an anti-baldness product caused the positive test result. *Los Angeles Times*. Retrieved from http://articles.latimes.com/2006/feb/11/sports/sp-lund11

Adair, L. (2011). In a league of their own: The case for intersex athletes. *Sports Law Journal, 18*, 121–151.

ADR Group. (2000). *Alternative dispute resolution: Explanatory booklet*. Bristol: ADR Group.

Agamben, G. (2005). *State of exception*. Chicago: University of Chicago Press.

Alexander, B. (2014). War on drugs redux: Welcome to the war on doping in sports. *Substance Use & Misuse, 49*(9), 1190–1193.

Allen, K. (July 31, 2016). How the practice of sex-testing targets female Olympic athletes: The IOC's pursuit of competitive fairness through testosterone, genitalia and sex testing is all wrong. *The Toronto Star*. Retrieved from https://www.thestar.com/news/world/2016/07/31/why-the-olympics-cant-figure-out-who-is-a-man-and-who-is-a-woman.html

Attorney General's Reference [No.6 of 1980] Q.B. 715.

Atyeo, D. (1981). *Violence in sports*. New York: Van Nontrand Reinhold Company.

Badenhausen, K. (January 22, 2014). As Stern says goodbye, Knicks, Lakers set records as NBA's most valuable teams. *Forbes*. Retrieved from http://www.forbes.com/sites/kurtbadenhausen/2014/01/22/as-stern-says-goodbye-knicks-lakers-set-records-as-nbas-most-valuable-teams/#27a30b80b88b

Baker, R., & Esherick, C. (2013). *Fundamentals of sports management*. Champaign, IL: Human Kinetics.

Barnes, J. (1996). *Sport and the law in Canada, 3rd edition*. Toronto: Butterworths.

Bateup, H. S., Booth, A., Shirtcliff, E. A., & Granger, D. A. (2002). Testosterone, cortisol, and women's competition. *Evolution and Human Behavior, 23*, 181–192.

Bandura, A. (1971). Vicarious and self-reinforcement processes. In R. Glaser (Ed.), *The nature of reinforcement* (pp. 228–278). New York: Academic Press.

Bandura, A. (1973). *Aggression: A social learning analysis*. Englewood Cliffs, NJ: Prentice-Hall.

Bandura, A. (1977). *Social Learning Theory*. Englewood Cliffs, NJ: Prentice-Hall.

Bandura, A. (1978). Social learning theory of aggression. *Journal of Communication, 28*, 12–29.

Barnes, J. (1996). *Sport and the law in Canada, 3rd edition.* Toronto: Butterworths.

Barnes, J. (2010). *The law of hockey.* Markham, ON: LexisNexis.

Barnes, R. (2007). *What is sport?* New Haven, CT: Yale University Press.

Baxter v. IOC. [2002] CAS 2002/A/376.

Becker, H. (1963). *Outsiders: Studies in the sociology of deviance.* New York: Free Press.

Beijing Declaration and Platform for Action. Retrieved from http://www.un.org/womenwatch/daw/beijing/platform/

Beloff, M. (2012). Is there a lex sportiva? In R. Siekmann & J. Soek (Eds.), *Lex sportiva: What is sports law?* (pp. 69–89). The Hague: TMC Asser Press.

Berkowitz, S. (May 13, 2016). NCAA asks Supreme Court to hear O'Bannon antitrust case. *USA Today.* Retrieved from http://www.usatoday.com/story/sports/college/2016/05/13/ncaa-asks-supreme-court-hear-obannon-antitrust-case/84341682/

Blackless, M., Charuvastra, A., Derryck, A., Fausto-Sterling, A., Lauzanne, K., & Lee, E. (2000). How sexually dimorphic are we? Review and synthesis. *Journal of Human Biology, 12,* 151–166.

Blackshaw, I. (2002). *Mediating sports disputes: National and international perspectives.* The Hague: TMC Asser Press.

Blackshaw, I. (2008a). Jail players who commit dangerous tackles, *International Sports Law Journal,* 1(2), 102–109.

Blackshaw, I. (2008b). Mediating business and sports disputes in Europe. *Entertainment and Sports Law Journal,* 6(2), 1–5.

Bodansky, B. (2013). Kicking the penalty: Why the European Court of Justice should allow salary caps in UEFA. *Fordham International Law Journal, 36,* 163–197.

Bradford, M. (2005). Sport, gender and law. *International Sports Law Journal, 1*(2), 78–83.

Brighton Declaration of Women in Sport. (2012). Retrieved from http://www.sportsbiz.bz/womensportinternational/conferences/brighton_declaration.htm

Britain, I. (2009). *The Paralympic Games explained.* New York: Routledge.

Brown, J. C., Verhagen, E., Knol, D., Van Mechelen, W., & Lambert, M. I. (2015). The effectiveness of the nationwide BokSmart rugby injury prevention program on catastrophic injury rates. *Scandinavian Journal of Medicine and Science in Sports*. http://dx.doi.org/doi:10.1111/sms.12414

Brown, M. (December 10, 2014). Major League Baseball sees record $9 billion in revenues for 2014. *Forbes*. Retrieved from http://www.forbes.com/sites/maurybrown/2014/12/10/major-league-baseball-sees-record-9-billion-in-revenues-for-2014/#38ec3cb76cb2

Bryant, J., Cominsky, P., & Zillman, D. (1977). Drama in sports commentary. *Journal of Communication, 27*(3), 140–149.

Bryant, J., Cominsky, P., & Zillman, D. (1981). The appeal of rough-and-tumble play in televised professional football. *Communication Quarterly, 29*, 256–262.

Bryant, J., Brown, D., Cominsky, P., & Zillman, D. (1982). Sports and spectators: Commentary and appreciation. *Journal of Communication, 32*, 109–119.

Burgess, R., & Akers, R. (1966). A differential association-reinforcement theory of criminal behavior. *Social Problems, 14*(2), 128–147.

Burstyn, V. (1999). *The rites of men: Manhood, politics, and the rites of men.* Toronto: University of Toronto Press.

Cabot, A. N., & Csoka, L. V. (2007). Fantasy sports: One form of mainstream wagering in the United States. *The John Marshall Law Review, 40*(4), 1195–1219.

Camporesi, S., & Maugeri, P. (2016). Unfair advantage and the myth of the level playing field in IAAF and IOC policies on hyperandrogenism: When is it fair to be a woman? In S. Montanola & A. Olivesi (Eds.) *Gender testing in sports: Ethics, cases, and controversies* (pp. 46–59). London: Routledge.

Carrigan, T., Connell, R., & Lee, J. (1985). Toward a new sociology of masculinity. *Theory and Society, 14*(5), 551–604.

CAS. (2015). Frequently asked questions. Retrieved from http://www.tas-cas.org/en/general-information/frequently-asked-questions.html

Central Council of Physical Recreation (1995). The Law Commission consultation paper No. 134 criminal law—Consent and offences against the person: A response on the issues for sports and games. *Sport and Law Journal, 3*, 47–60.

Cernec, J. (2012). Fair trial guarantees before the court of arbitration for sport. *Human Rights and International Legal Discourse, 6*(2), 259–283.

Coakley, J. (1998). *Sports in society: Issues and controversies*. Boston, MA: McGraw-Hill.

Coakley, J., & Donnelly, P. (2004/2009). *Sports in society: Issues and controversies, Canadian edition*. Toronto: McGraw-Hill.

Coalition for the Inclusion of Athletes in Sport. (2016). *The guiding principles for inclusion in sport*. Retrieved from http://www.playthegame.org/fileadmin/documents/recoinclusivesportcp2.pdf

Collective Bargaining Agreement between the National Basketball Association (NBA) and the National Basketball Players Association (NBPA). (2001). Retrieved from http://www.nba.com/media/CBA101.pdf

Commission of the European Communities. (2007). White Paper on Sport. Retrieved from http://eur-lex.europa.eu/legal-content/EN/TXT/?uri=CELEX%3A52007DC0391

Conn, D. (September 28, 2015). Sepp Blatter and Michel Platini deny wrongdoing over £1.35m payment. *The Guardian*. Retrieved from https://www.theguardian.com/football/2015/sep/28/sepp-blatter-fifa-returns-to-work-michel-platini

Connell, R., & Messerschmidt, J. (2005). Hegemonic masculinity: Rethinking the concept. *Gender & Society, 19*, 829–859.

Cooper, E. (2010). Gender testing in athletic competitions—Human rights violations: Why Michael Phelps is praised and Caster Semenya is chastised. *Gender, Race & Justice, 14*, 233–264.

Corbett, R. (2003). Resolving disputes through negotiation. *Coaches Report, 10*(1), Retrieved from http://www.sportlaw.ca/2003/02/resolving-disputes-through-negotiation/

Corbett, R., Findlay, H., & Lech, D. (2008). *Legal issues in sport: Tools and techniques for the sport manager*. Toronto: Edmond Montgomery Publications.

Cottrell, S. (2010). Freedom of religion and rules of safety. *World Sports Law Report, 8*(2), 12–16.

Crown Prosecution Service. (2015). *Offences against the person, incorporating the charging standard*. Retrieved from http://www.cps.gov.uk/legal/l_to_o/offences_against_the_person/

Davies, C. (2012). Labour market controls and sport in light of UEFA's Financial Fair Play Regulations, *European Competition Law Review, 33*(10), 443.

De Kruif, P. (1945). *The male hormone*. Garden City, NY: Garden City Publishing, 1945.

Decision [2000] Football World Cup OJ 2000 L5/55.

Declaration on Sport in the Treaty of Amsterdam. (1997). Retrieved from http://www.europarl.europa.eu/topics/treaty/pdf/amst-en.pdf

Declaration on Sport in the Treaty of Nice. (2000). Retrieved from http://ec.europa.eu/competition/sectors/sports/policy.html

Deliège v Ligue francophone de judo et disciplines associées ASBL, Ligue belge de judo ASBL, Union européenne de judo [2000] C-51/96.

Denhart, C. (August 7, 2013). How the $1.2 trillion college debt crisis is crippling students, parents and the economy. *Forbes*. Retrieved from http://www.forbes.com/sites/specialfeatures/2013/08/07/how-the-college-debt-is-crippling-students-parents-and-the-economy/#2beff7741a41

Deutscher Handballbund v Kolpak [2003] ECR I4135.

Dimeo, P. (2007) *A history of drug use in sport, 1876–1976: Beyond good and evil*, London: Routledge.

DiNicola, R. A., & Mendeloff, S. (1983). Controlling violence in professional sports: Rule reform and the Federal Professional Sports Violence Commission. *Duquesne Law Review*, *21*(4), 843–916.

Dixon, M., Ghezzi, P., Lyons, C., & Wilson, G. (Eds.) (2006). *Gambling: Behavior theory, research, and application*. Oxford: New Harbinger Publications.

Doig, P., Lloyd-Smith, R., Prior, J., & Sinclair, D. (1997). Position statement: Sex testing (gender verification) in sport. *Canadian Academy of Sports Medicine*. Retrieved from www.casm-acms.org/forms/statements/GenderVerifEng.pdf

Dollard, J., Doob, L., Miller, N., Mowrer, O., & Sears, R. (1939). *Frustration and aggression*. New Haven, CT: Yale University Press.

Dona v. Mantero [1976] ECR 1333, 2 CMLR 578, ECJ.

Donnellan, L. (2010). *Sport and the law: A concise guide*. Dublin: Blackhall Publishing.

Downes, S., & Mackay, D. (1996). *Running scared: How athletics lost its innocence*. Edinburgh: Mainstream.

Duke University. (2008). *Unrivaled ambition: A strategic plan for athletics*. Durham, NC: Duke University. Retrieved from http://today.duke.edu/showcase/reports/athleticsstrategyfinal.pdf

Dunn v. University of Ottawa [1995] O.J. 2856.

Dunning, E. (1999). *Sport matters: Sociological studies of sport, violence, and civilization*. London: Routledge.

Edelman, M. (Jan. 6, 2014), The case for paying college athletes. *U.S. News*. Retrieved from http://www.usnews.com/opinion/articles/2014/01/06/ncaa-college-athletes-should-be-paid

Edwards v. BAF and IAAF [1998] 2 CMLR 363.

Egger, G. (1990). *Sports injuries in Australia: Causes, costs and prevention*. Sydney: Centre for Health Promotion and Research.

Emamdjomeh, A., & Bensinger, K. (February 1, 2014). Publicity from a fight over state law prompts players across the country to file more than 1,000 injury claims before a September deadline; that could cost top pro sports leagues hundreds of millions. *Los Angeles Times*. Retrieved from http://www.latimes.com/business/la-fi-nfl-claims-20140201-dto-htmlstory.html

Enderby Town FC v. The Football Association [1971] 1 All ER 215.

Epstein, A. (2002). ADR in sport management. *Journal of Legal Aspects of Sport*, *12*(3), 154–182.

Epstein, A. (2013). *Sports law*. Mason, OH: Cengage Learning.

Equity Act. (2010). Retrieved from http://www.legislation.gov.uk/ukpga/2010/15/contents

Erickson, K. (1966). *Wayward puritans: A study in the sociology of deviance*. New York: Wiley.

Eugene, D., & Gibson, N. (1980). Violence in professional sports: A proposal for self-regulation. *Communication and Education Law Journal*, *3*, 425–453.

European Gaming & Betting Association (2015). The economic synergy between sports and sport betting. *EGBA Newsletter*, *19*, 1–4.

Fafinski, S. (2005). Consent and the rules of the game: The interplay of civil and criminal liability for sporting injuries. *Journal of Criminal Law*, *69*(5), 414–426.

Farrey, T. (May 31, 2014). Players, game makers settle for $40M. *ESPN*. Retrieved from http://espn.go.com/espn/otl/story/_/id/11010455/college-athletes-reach-40-million-settlement-ea-sports-ncaa-licensing-arm

FC Shaktar Donetsk v. Matuzalém Francelino da Silva, Real Zaragoza and FIFA [2008] A/1519 and 1520.

FIDE (2015). FIDE anti-doping rules based on WADA's models of best practice for international federations and the World Anti-Doping Code. Retrieved from https://www.fide.com/FIDE/handbook/FIDEAntiDopingRules.pdf

References

Fogel, C. (2013a). *Game-day gangsters: Crime and deviance in Canadian football.* Edmonton, AB: Athabasca University Press.

Fogel, C. (2013b). Bio-medical wars in Canadian sport: Issues in the prevention and detection of anabolic steroid use. *Journal of Physical Education and Sport, 13*(3), 283–286.

Forbes, G., Adams-Curtis, L., Pakalka, A., White, K. (2006). Dating aggression, sexual coercion, and aggression-supporting attitudes among college men as a function of participation in aggressive high school sports. *Violence Against Women, 12,* 441–455.

Freud, S. (1922). *Beyond the pleasure principle.* Translated by C. J. M. Hubback. Vienna: Psycho-Analytical Press.

Fuller, C. W. (2008). Catastrophic injury in rugby union: is the level of risk acceptable? *Sports Medicine, 38*(12), 975–986.

Gardiner, S. (1994). The law and the sports field. *Criminal Law Review, 1,* 513–515.

Gardiner, S., & Felix, A. (1995). Juridification of the football field: Strategies for giving law the elbow, *Marquette Sports Law Review, 5,* 189–220.

Gardiner, S., & James, M. (1997). Touchlines and guidelines: The Lord Advocate's response to sportsfield violence, *Criminal Law Review, 1,* 41–45.

Gardiner, A., James, M., O'Leary, J., & Welch, R. (2006). *Sports Law 3rd Edition.* London: Cavendish Publishing.

Gardiner, S. (2007). Sports participation and criminal liability. *Sport and Law Journal, 15,* 19–29.

Garrett v. Canadian Weightlifting Federation [1990] Unreported decision of the Alta QB (Edmonton), Case No. 9003-0122.

Gandert, D., Bae, A., Woerner, T., Meece, T. (2013). The intersection of women's Olympic sport and intersex athletes: A long and winding road. *Indiana Law Review, 46,* 387–423.

Geeraert, A., & Mrkonjic, M. (2014). A rationalist perspective on the autonomy of international sport governing bodies: towards a pragmatic autonomy in the steering of sports. *International Journal of Sport Policy and Politics, 7*(4), 473–488.

Glazer, S. (2012). Sporting chance: Litigating sexism out of the Olympic intersex policy. *Journal of Law & Policy, 20,* 545–580.

Gleaves, J., & Llewellyn, M. (2014). Sport, drugs, and amateurism: Tracing the real cultural origins of anti-doping rules in international sport. *International Journal for the History of Sport, 31*(8), 839–853.

Goldberg, S., Frank, E., & Rogers, N. (1992). *Dispute resolution: Negotiation, mediation, and other processes, 2nd ed.* Boston: Little, Brown and Company.

Goldstein, J. (1998). *Why we watch: The attractions of violent entertainment.* Oxford University Press.

Grayson, E. (1971). On the field of play. *New Law Journal, 121,* 413.

Grayson, E. (1988). The day sport dies. *New Law Journal, 138,* 9.

Grayson, E. (1990). Keeping sport alive. *New Law Journal, 140,* 12.

Grayson, E. (1991). Foul play. *New Law Journal. 141.* 742.

Grayson, E., & Bond, C. (1993). Making foul play a crime. *Solicitors Journal, 1,* 693.

Grayson, E. (1994) Drake's drum beat for sporting remedies/injuries. *New Law Journal, 144,* 1094.

Grayson, E. (1999). *Sport and the law 3rd edition.* London: Buttersworth.

Greenberg, J. (1999). Defining male and female: Intersexuality and the collision between law and biology. *Arizona Law Review, 41,* 265–328.

Greenberg, J. (2012). *Intersexuality and the law: Why sex matter.* New York: New York University Press.

Geey, D. (2011). The UEFA Financial Fair Play rules: A difficult balancing act. *Entertainment and Sports Law Journal, 9,* 50–57.

Gulotta, S. (1980). Torts in sports: Deterring violence in professional athletics. *Fordham Law Review, 48*(5), 764–793.

Gunn, M. (1998). Impact of the law on sport with specific reference to the way sport is played. *Contemporary Legal Issues, 3*(4), 212.

Hart v. Elec. Arts, Inc. [2013] 717 F.3d 141, 145.

Haslip, S. (2001). International sports law perspective: A consideration of the need for a national dispute resolution system for national sport organizations in Canada. *Marquette Sports Law Review, 11,* 245–274.

Hauge, J. (2012). Incentive for aggression in American football. In R. T. Jewell (Ed.) *Violence and aggression in sporting contests: Economics, history, and policy* (pp. 29–46). New York: Springer.

Healy, D. (2009). *Sport and the law, fourth edition.* Sydney: University of New South Wales University Press.

Heitner, D. (June 9, 2014). NCAA settles Electronic Arts video game lawsuit for $20 million. *Forbes.* Retrieved from http://www.forbes.com/sites/darrenheitner/2014/06/09/ncaa-settles-electronic-arts-video-game-lawsuit-for-20-million/#24e5cd16521c

Helsinki Report on Sport. (1999). Retrieved from http://eur-lex.europa.eu/LexUriServ/LexUriServ.do?uri=COM:1999:0644:FIN:EN:PDF

Hermann, A., & Henneberg, M. (August 4, 2013). Exposing dopers in sport: Is it really worth the cost, *The Conversation*, Retrieved from http://theconversation.com/exposing-dopers-in-sport-is-it-really-worth-the-cost-16464

Hill, D. (2010). *The fix: Soccer and organized crime.* Toronto: McClelland & Stewart.

Holden, C. (2004). An everlasting gender gap? *Science, 305*(5684), 639–640.

Hollande. (March 8, 2013). Francoise Hollande wants 75% company tax on salaries over 1m Euros. *The Guardian.* Retrieved from www.theguardian.com/world/2013/mar/28/francoise-hollande-tax-salaries

Holt, R. (1992). Amateurism and its interpretation: The social origins of British sport. *Innovation, 5*(4), 19–31.

Hornsby, S. (2001). Financial rules: UEFA FFPR Regulations: the grounds for legal challenge. *World Sports Law Report, 9*(3), 1.

Houlihan, B. (1999). Anti-doping policy in sport: The politics of international policy coordination. *Public Administration, 77*(2), 311–335.

Hughes, R., & Coakley, J. (1991). Positive deviance among athletes: The implications of over-conformity to the sport ethic. *Sociology of Sport Journal,* 8(4), 307–325.

Huma, R., & Staurowsky, E. J. (2012). The price of poverty in big time college sports. *National College Players Association.* Retrieved from http://www.ncpanow.org/research/body/The-Price-of-Poverty-in-Big-Time-College-Sport.pdf

Humphrey v. Viacom, Inc. [2007]. No. 06-2768, 2007 WL 1797648.

Hunt, T. (2011). *Drug games: The International Olympic Committee and the politics of doping, 1960–2008.* Austin: University of Texas Press.

Hurst, M. (September 11, 2009). Caster Semenya has male sex organs and no womb or ovaries. *Daily Telegraph.* Retrieved from www.dailytelegraph.com.au/sport/semenya-has-no-womb-or-ovaries

Hutchins, B., & Phillips, M. (1998). Selling permissible violence: The commodification of Australian Rugby League 1970–1995. *International Review of the Sociology of Sport, 34*, 246–263.

Hytner, D. (September 1, 2013). Gareth Bayle transfer: Real Madrid confirm signing in reported €100m deal. *The Guardian*. Retrieved from https://www.theguardian.com/football/2013/sep/01/gareth-bale-real-madrid-tottenham

Illegal Gambling Business Act. (1955). 18 U.S.C.

In re NCAA Student-Athlete Name & Likeness Litig. [2011] C 09-1967 CW, 2011 WL 1642256.

International Association of Athletic Federations. (2011). HA regulations: Explanatory notes. Retrieved from www.iaaf.org/about-iaaf/documents/medical

International Charter on Physical Education and Sport. (1978). Retrieved from http://portal.unesco.org/en/ev.php-URL_ID=13150&URL_DO=DO_TOPIC&URL_SECTION=201.html

International Olympic Committee (2012) IOC Regulations on Female Hyperandrogenism. Retrieved from http://www.olympic.org/Documents/Commissions_PDFfiles/Medical_commission/2012-06-22-IOC-Regulations-on-Female-Hyperandrogenism-eng.pdf

International Olympic Committee. (2013). Olympic Charter: Fundamental principles of olympism. Retrieved from http://www.olympic.org/documents/olympic_charter_en.pdf

Intersex Society of North America. (N.D.). Intersex conditions. Retrieved from http://www.isna.org/faq/conditions

Irvine v. Royal Burgess Golfing Society of Edinburgh [2004] SCLR 386.

James, M. (2013). *Sports law*. New York: Palgrave Macmillan.

Jasthi, S. (March 3, 2015). March Madness? Top NCAA players worth $488,000. *NerdWallet*. Retrieved from https://www.nerdwallet.com/blog/cities/data-studies/ncaa-players-worth-2015-march-madness/

Jewell, R. T. (2012). Aggressive play and demand for English Premier League football. In R. T. Jewell (Ed.) *Violence and aggression in sporting contests: Economics, history, and policy* (pp. 29–46). New York: Springer.

Johnson, G. (2008). NFL players' union takes hit it court. *Los Angeles Times*. Retrieved from http://articles.latimes.com

Johnson, W. O., & Moore, K. (1988). The loser. *Sports Illustrated*.

Jones v. Welsh Rugby Football Union [1997]. EWCA Civ 3066.

Kaplan, D. (March 9, 2015). NFL projecting revenue increase of $1B over 2014. *Sport Business Daily*. Retrieved from http://www.sportsbusinessdaily.com/Journal/Issues/2015/03/09/Leagues-and-Governing-Bodies/NFL-revenue.aspx

Katz, J. (1996). Masculinity and sports culture. In R. E. Lapchick (Ed.) *Sport in society: Equal opportunity or business as usual?* (pp. 101–106) Thousand Oaks, CA: Sage.

Kehrli, K. (2014). The unspecified specificity of sport: A proposed solution to the European Court of Justice's treatment of the specificity of sport. *Brooklyn Journal of International Law, 39*, 403–441.

Keller v. Elec. Arts, Inc., [2010] No. C 09-1967 CW, WL 530108.

Kemper, K. E. (2009). *College football and American culture in the cold war era: Waging the cold war's ideological battles on the gridiron.* Champaign, IL: University of Illinois Press.

Keogh, F. (2014). FIFA Women's World Cup: Host Canada refuses pitch talks. BBC Sport. Retrieved from http://www.bbc.com/sport/0/football/29986115

Kilb, S. (2014). Fixing financial fair play: How to make European soccer's salary cap stick. *Indonesian Journal of International & Comparative Law, 1*(3), 808–842.

King, J. (May 23, 2009). AAU basketball, greed, and its effect on the NBA. *Bleacher Report*. Retrieved from http://bleacherreport.com/articles/182342-aau-basketball-greed-and-its-effect-on-the-nba

Knight, R. (2013). A football monopoly: The lack of parity and financial responsibility in today's game. *ILSA Journal of International & Comparative Law, 7*, 107–120.

Kuntz, M. (2006). 265 million playing football. *FIFA Magazine*. Retrieved from http://www.fifa.com/mm/document/fifafacts/bcoffsurv/emaga_9384_10704.pdf

Kuper, S., & Szymanski, S. (2009). *Soccernomics: Why England loses, why Germany and Brazil win, and why the US, Japan, Australia, Turkey—and Even Iraq—are destined to become the kings of the world's most popular sport.* New York: Nation Books.

La Rocco, C. (2004). Rings of power: Peter Ueberroth and the 1984 Los Angeles Olympic Games. *Financial History*. Retrieved from www.financialhistory.org

Langone v. Patrick Kaiser & Fanduel, Inc. [2013] No. 12 C 2073, 2013 U.S. Dist. LEXIS 145941.

Large, D. C. (2007). *Nazi games: The Olympics of 1936*. New York: Norton.

Laquer, T. (1990). *Making sex: Body and gender from the Greeks to Freud*. Cambridge, MA: Harvard University Press.

LaVoi, N. M., & Kane, M. J. (2011). Sociological aspects of sport. In P. Pedersen, J. Parks, J. Quarterman & L. Thibault (Eds.), *Contemporary Sport Management (4th ed)* (pp. 372–391) Champaign, IL: Human Kinetics.

Lehtonen and others v. Federation Royale Belge de Societies de basketball [1996] ASBL C-176.

Leizman, J. (1999). *Let's kill' em: Understanding and controlling violence in sports*. Lanham, MD: University Press of America.

Leutgeb, V., Leitner, M., Wabnegger, A., Klug, D., Scharmuller, W., Zussner, T., & Schienle, A. (2015). Brain abnormalities in high-risk violent offenders and their association with psychopathic traits and criminal recidivism. *Neuroscience, 308*, 194–201.

Lindholm, J. (2010). The problem with salary caps under European Union law. *Texas Review of Entertainment and Sports Law, 12*(2), 189–213.

Long, C. (2012). Promoting competition or preventing it? A Competition Law analysis of UEFA's Financial Fair Play Rules. *Marquette Sports Law Review, 23*, 75–101.

Lorenz, K. (1963). *On aggression*. New York: Harcourt, Brace and World.

Madden, P. (2012). Welfare economics of Financial Fair Play in a sports league with benefactor owners. University of Manchester Economics Discussion Paper Series.

Maennig, W. (2002). On the economics of doping and corruption in International sports, *Journal of Sports Economics, 3*(1), 2002, 61–89.

Matuzalém v. FIFA and CAS [2009] Decision 4A.320.

Matuzalém v. FIFA and CAS [2011] Unreported, June 29.

Matuzalém v. FIFA and CAS [2012] Decision 4A.558.

McArdle, D. (2015). *Dispute resolution in sport: Athletes, law and arbitration*. New York: Routledge.

McInnes v. Onslow-Fane [1978] 1 WLR 1520.

McLaren, R. (1998). A new order: Athletes' rights and the Court of Arbitration at theOlympic Games. *Olympika: The International Journal of Olympic Studies, 7,* 1–24.

McLaren, R. (2001). The Court of Arbitration for Sport: An independent arena for the world's sports disputes. *Valparaiso University Law Review, 35*(2), 379–405.

McMurphy, B. (October 4, 2016). Louisville bans Lamar Jackson, other athletes from signing autographs. *ABC News*. Retrieved from http://abcnews.go.com/Sports/louisville-bans-lamar-jackson-athletes-signing-autographs/story?id=42570157

Meca-Medina & Majcen v. Commission of the European Communities [2006] 5 CMLR 18.

Messner, M. (1992). *Power at play: Sports and the problem of masculinity.* Boston, MA: Beacon Press.

Messner, M. (2002). *Taking the field: Women, men, and sport.* Minneapolis: University of Minnesota Press.

Mestre, M. (2013). Player contracts: The 'Striani case': UEFA's 'break-even rule' & EU law. *World Sports Law Report, 11*(7), 1.

Miah, A. (2004). *Genetically modified athletes: Biomedical ethics, gene doping and sport.* New York: Routledge.

Miami Dolphins v. Williams [2005] 365 F.Supp. 2d 1301.

Michigan Law Review Association (1976). Consent in criminal law: Violence in sports. *Michigan Law Review, 75*(1), 148–179.

Modahl v. British Athletics Federation Ltd [2001] WL 1135166.

Moore, C. (1997). *Sports law and litigation.* Birmingham, CLT Professional Publishing.

Morrow, S. (2013). Football club financial reporting: Time for a new model? *Sport, Business, and Management: An International Journal, 3*(4), 297–311.

Morrow, S. (2015). Power and logics in Scottish football: the financial collapse of Rangers FC. *Sport, Business, and Management: An International Journal, 5*(4), 325–343.

Mottram, D. (2005). *Drugs in sports.* London: Routledge.

Muir, K., & Seitz, T. (2004). Machismo, misogyny, and homophobia in a male athletic subculture: A participant- observation study of deviant rituals in collegiate rugby. *Deviant Behavior, 25,* 303–327.

Muller, J. C., Lammert, J., & Hovemann, G. (2012). The Financial Fair Play Regulations of UEFA: An adequate concept to ensure the long-term viability and sustainability of European club football? *International Journal of Sport Finance, 7,* 117–140.

Naam, R. (2005). *More than human: Embracing the promise of biological enhancement,* New York: Broadway Books.

Nafzinger, J. (2004). *International sports law, 2nd edition.* New York: Transnational Law Publishers.

National Football League Players v. Pro-Football [1994] 857 F. Supp. 71.

NCAA (2013). Retrieved from http://grfx.cstv.com/photos/schools/usc/genrel/auto_pdf/2013-14/misc_non_event/ncaa-manual.pdf

NFHS. (August 13, 2015). High school sports participation increases for 26th consecutive year. *National Federation of State High School Associations.* Retrieved from https://www.nfhs.org/articles/high-school-sports-participation-increases-for-26th-consecutive-year/

Nicoliello, M., & Zampatti, D. (2016). Football clubs' profitability after the Financial Fair Play Regulation: evidence from Italy. *Sport, Business and Management: An International Journal, 6*(4), http://dx.doi.org/10.1108/SBM-07-2014-0037

O'Bannon v. Nat'l Collegiate Athletic Ass'n [2014] No. C 09-3329 CW, WL 3899815, 962–63.

O'Connell, S., & Manschreck, T. (2012). Playing through the pain: Psychiatric risks among athletes. *Current Psychiatry, 11*(2). Retrieved from http://www.currentpsychiatry.com/index.php?id=22661&tx_ttnews[tt_news]=176934

Oakley, A. (2015). *Sex, gender, and society.* Farnham, UK: Ashgate Publishing.

Ohuruogu v. UK Athletics Limited (UKA) & International Association of Athletics Federations (IAAF) [2006] Arbitration CAS 2006/A/1165.

Omerod, D. C. (2005). Case comment—Contact sports: Application of defence of consent. *Criminal Law Review,* 381–384.

Pendlebury, A. (2006). Perceptions of playing culture in sport: The problem of diverse opinion in the light of Barnes. *Entertainment and Sports Law Journal, 4,* 1–7.

Pendlebury, A. (2012). On the ball violence: Challenges in court. *Entertainment and Sports Law Journal, 10,* 1–9.

Pechstein v. International Skating Union [2009] CAS 2009/A/1912.

People v. Turner [1995] 629 N.Y.S. 2d 661.

Pereira, H., Marques, M., Talhas, I., & Neto, F. (2004). Incidental clostebol contamination in athletes after sexual intercourse. *Clinical Chemistry*, *50*(2), 456–457.

Peterson, A. (2010). But she doesn't run like a girl...: The ethic of fair play and the flexibility of the binary conception of sex. *Tulane Journal of International & Comparative Law*, *19*, 315–330.

Pieper, L. (2016). *Sex testing: Gender policing in women's sports*. Urbana: University of Illinois Press.

Proctor, B. (2012). When should criminal liability be attached to harmful challenges in football? *Student Journal of Law*. Retrieved from http://www.sjol.co.uk/issue-3/criminal-football

Professional and Amateur Sports Protection Act (1992). 28 U.S.C.

R. v. Barnes [2004] EWCA 3246.

R. v. Bertuzzi [2004] B.C.J. 2692.

R. v. Best [2004] Unreported.

R. v. Bishop [1986] Unreported.

R. v. Billinghurst [1978] 22 Criminal Law Review 553.

R. v. Bowyer [2002] 1 Cr App R (S) 448.

R. v. Bradshaw [1878] 14 Cox's CC 83.

R. v. Brown [1993] 2 Weekly Law Report 556.

R. v. Calton [1999] 2 Cr App R(S) 64.

R. v. CC [2009] ONCJ 249.

R. v. Cey [1989] 48 CCC (3d) 480.

R. v. Collins [1994] Unreported.

R v Coney [1882] 8 QBD 534.

R. v. Deverereux [1996]. Unreported.

R. v. Evans [2010] Unreported.

R. v. Garfield [2007] EWCA Crim 2456.

R. v. Gingell [1980] 25 Criminal Law Review 661.

R. v. Goodwin [1995] 16 Cr. App. R.(S.) 885.

R. v. Hardy [1994] Unreported.

R. v. Henderson [1976] 5 W.W.R. 119.

R. v. Johnson [1986] 8 Cr App R(S) 343.

R. v. Lloyd [1989] 11 Cr App R(S) 36.

R. v. Marsh [1994]. Unreported.

R. v. McSorley [2000] BCJ 1993.

R. v. Moss [2000] 1 Cr App R (S) 307.

R. v. O'Callaghan [2015] Unreported.

R. v. Pepper [2002] EWCA Crim 3141.

R. v. Powell [2001] Unreported.

R. v. Rees [1992] Unreported.

R. v. Unsworth [2013] Unreported.

Reeb, M. (2006). The role and functions of the Court of Arbitration for Sport (CAS). In I. Blackshaw, R. Siekmann, & J. Soek (Eds), *The Court of Arbitration for Sport 1984–2004*. The Hague: TMC Asser Press.

Reeser, J. C. (2005). Gender, identity, and sport: Is it a level playing field? *British Journal of Sports Medicine, 39*(10), 553–56.

Reynolds v. IAAF [1994] 23F.3d 1110.

Ritchie, I. (2012). The 'spirit of sport': Understanding the cultural foundations of olympism through anti-doping policy. In the proceedings of the *Eleventh International Symposium for Olympic Research*. London, ON.

Ritchie, R., Reynard, J., & Lewis, T. (2008). Intersex and the Olympic games. *Journal of the Royal Society of Medicine, 101*, 395–399.

Roberts, S., & Palmer, M. (2005). *Dispute processes: ADR and the primary forms of decision-making*. Cambridge: Cambridge University Press.

Romero, M. (2015). Check to the head: The tragic death of NHL enforcer Derek Boogaard and the NHL's negligence—How enforcers are treated as second-class employees. *Jeffrey S. Moorad Sports Law Journal, 22*. Retrieved from http://digitalcommons.law.villanova.edu/mslj/vol22/iss1/7

Rosenberg, M. (August 26, 2010). Change is long overdue: College football players should be paid. *Sports Illustrated*. Retrieved from http://www.si.com/more-sports/2010/08/26/pay-college

Rugby Football History (2015). *1924 Paris Olympics*. Retrieved from http://www.rugbyfootballhistory.com/olympics.htm#1924

Ruiz, R. (June 7, 2016). Sports arbitration court ruling against German speedskater Claudia Pechstein is upheld. *The New York Times*. Retrieved from http://www.nytimes.com/2016/06/08/sports/sports-arbitration-court-ruling-against-german-speedskater-claudia-pechstein-is-upheld.html?_r=0

Rupert, J. L. (2011). Genitals to genes: The history and biology of gender verification in the Olympics. *CBMH, 28*(2), 339–365.

Sagen v. Vancouver Committee for the 2010 Olympic and Paralympic Games (VANOC). [2009] BCSC 942.

Seattle Times Co. v. Tielsch [1972] 80 Wash. 2d 502, 504.

Schubert, M. (2014). Potential agency problems in European club football? The case of UEFA Financial Fair Play. *Sport, Business, and Management: An International Journal, 4*(4), 336–350.

"Shamateurism" (August 28, 1995). Shamateurism's end: Taking the money and running. *The Guardian*.

Sheard, K., & Dunning, E. (1973). The rugby football club as a type of "male preserve": Some sociological notes. *International Review for the Sociology of Sport, 8*, 5–21.

Slaikeu, K. A., & Hasson, R. H. (1998). *Controlling the costs of conflict*. San Francisco: Jossey-Bass Publishers.

Smith, C. (December 22, 2015). College football's most valuable teams 2015. *Forbes*. Retrieved from http://www.forbes.com/sites/chrissmith/2015/12/22/college-footballs-most-valuable-teams-2015-texas-notre-dame-and-tennessee/#9c8380151300

Smith, J., & Willingham, M. (2015). *Cheated: The UNC scandal, the education of athletes, and the future of big-time college sports*. Lincoln, NE: University of Nebraska Press.

Smith, L. (1998). *Nike is a goddess: The history of women in sports*. New York: Atlantic Monthly Press.

Smith, M. (1983). *Violence and sport*. Toronto: Butterworth.

Smolden v. Whitworth [1997] E.L.R. 115.

Solomon, J. (August 14, 2013). EA Sports NCAA football video game trademarks: Who's in, who's out and who's on the fence. *All Alabama*. Retrieved from http://www.al.com/sports/index.ssf/2013/O8/whosinand_whos-outlicensing.html

Sport England. (2015). *Who plays sport*. Retrieved from http://www.sportengland.org/research/who-plays-sport/by-sport/

Standen, J. (2008). *Taking sports seriously: Law and sports in contemporary American culture*. Durham, NC: University of Carolina Press.

Standen, J. (2009). The manly sports: The problematic use of criminal law to regulate sports violence. *Journal of Criminal Law and Criminology, 3*, 619–642.

Staples, A. (October 29, 2014). Todd Gurley suspension ruling shows major problems with NCAA's system. *Sports Illustrated.* Retrieved from http://www.si.com/collegefootball/2014/10/29/todd-gurley-georgia-bulldogs-ncaa-suspension

Stein, M. (2011). David Stern: Season hangs in the balance. *ESPN.* Retrieved from http://espn.go.com/nba/story/_/id/7031637/nba-lockout-david-stern-threaten-cancellation-season-sources-say

Steinberg, L. (August 29, 2014). The fantasy football explosion. *Forbes.* Retrieved from http://www.forbes.com/sites/leighsteinberg/2014/08/29/the-fantasy-football-explosion/#5d92ca5f5458

Storm, R. (2012). The need for regulating professional soccer in Europe: A soft budget constraint approach argument. *Sport, Business, and Management: An International Journal, 2*(1), 21–38.

Strenk, A. (1988). Amateurism: The myth and the reality. In J. P. Segrave and D. Chu (eds.) *The Olympic Games in transition* (pp. 307–321). Champaign, IL: Human Kinetics.

Sterling v. Leeds Rugby League Cup [2001] ISLR 201.

Stochholm, K., Bojesen, A., Jensen, A., Juul, S., & Gravholt, C. (2012). Criminality in men with Klinefelter's syndrome and XYY syndrome: a cohort study. *British Medical Journal, 2.* Retrieved from http://bmjopen.bmj.com/content/2/1/e000650.full

Subramanian, P. (September 4, 2013). Surprising stats about fantasy sports. *Yahoo.* Retrieved from http://finance.yahoo.com/blogs/breakout/5-surprising-stats-fantasy-sports-154356461.html

Sutherland, E. (1947). *Principles of criminology.* Philadelphia: Lippincott.

Swarr, L., Gross, S., & Theron, L. (2009). South African intersex activism: Caster Semenya's impact and import. *Feminist Studies, 35*, 657–662.

Szymanski, S. (2012). Insolvency in English professional football: Irrational exuberance or negative shocks? Working Paper Series, Paper No. 12-02, International Association of Sports Economists & North American Association of Sports Economists.

Tarde, G. (1912). *Penal philosophy.* Boston: Little, Brown.

Taylor v. Moorabbin Saints Football League and Football Victoria [2004] VCAT 158.

Taylor, W. (1991). *Macho medicine: A history of the anabolic steroid epidemic*. Jefferson, NC: McFarland.

Thomas (Next friend of) v. Hamilton Board of Education [1994] O.J. 2444.

Thompson, M. J. (2001). Give me $25 on Red and Derek Jeter for $26: Do fantasy sports leagues constitute gambling? *Sports Lawyers Journal, 8*, 21–42.

"Time Warner." (April 22, 2010). Time Warner Joins CBS in $10.8 Billion March Madness TV Deal. *Fox Business*.

Todd, J., & Todd, T. (2001). Significant events in the history of drug testing and the Olympic movement: 1960–99. In W. Wilson & E. Derse (Eds.), *Doping in elite sport: The politics of drugs in the Olympic movement*. Champaign, IL: Human Kinetics.

Todd, T. (1992). A history of the use of steroids in sport. In J. Berryman & R. Park (Eds.), *Sport and exercise science: Essays in the history of sports medicine* (pp. 319–350). Urbana: University of Illinois Press.

Treaty on the Functioning of the European Union. Retrieved from http://eur-lex.europa.eu/legal-content/EN/TXT/?uri=CELEX:12012E/TXT

Trimdas, T. (2006). *The general principles of EU law*. Oxford: Oxford University Press.

Turner, J. N. (1996). A history of sport and law in Australia. *Sporting Traditions, 2*(2), 176–190.

Turner, J. (2016). Transgender athletes are unfair to women. *The Times*. Retrieved from http://www.thetimes.co.uk/tto/opinion/columnists/article4676154.ece

Quigley v. UID [1994] CAS 94.

UEFA. (2011). Financial Fair Play. Union of European Football Associations. Retrieved from http://www.uefa.com/MultimediaFiles/Download/Tech/uefaorg/General/01/80/54/10/1805410_DOWNLOAD.pdf

Underwood, J. (1984). *Spoiled sport: A fan's notes on the troubles of spectator sports*. Boston: Little, Brown and Company.

United Nations. (1948). Universal Declaration of Human Rights. Retrieved from http://www.un.org/en/documents/udhr/

United Nations. (1979). Convention on the Elimination of All Forms of Discrimination Against Women. Retrieved from http://www.un.org/womenwatch/daw/cedaw/

United Nations (2014). Sport for development and peace. Retrieved from http://www.un.org/ga/search/view_doc.asp?symbol=A/69/L.5

Unlawful Internet Gambling Enforcement Act. (2006). H.R. 4411, 109th Cong. (2d Sess. 2006).

URBSFA v. Bosman, 1995 E.C.R. I-4921.

Uthman, D. (June 5, 2014). John Calipari, Kentucky agree to $52 million contract extension. *USA Today*. Retrieved from http://www.usatoday.com/story/sports/ncaab/sec/2014/06/05/univeristy-of-kentucky-john-calipari-contract-extension-seven-years-52-million/10038673/

Valkenburg, D., De Hon, O., & Van Hilvoorde, I. (2014). Doping control, providing whereabouts and the importance of privacy for elite athletes. *International Journal of Drug Policy, 25*(2), 212–218.

Van Noll, W. (July 25, 2014). All leagues share revenue, but NFL is best at it. *The Field of Green*. Retrieved from http://thefieldsofgreen.com/2014/07/25/all-leagues-share-revenue-but-the-nfl-is-by-far-the-best-at-it/

Varis v IBU [2008] CAS 1607.

Vernonia School District 47J v. Acton [1995] 515 U.S. 646.

Voicu, A. (2005). Civil liability arising from breaches of sports regulations. *The International Sports Law Journal, 1*(2), 22–23.

Vowles v. Evans [2003] W.L.R. 1607.

Voy, R., & Deeter, K. (1991). *Drugs, sport, and politics*. Champaign, IL: Leisure Press, 1991.

WADA v ITF & Gasquet [2009] CAS 1930.

Waddington, I. (2010). Surveillance and control in sport: A sociologist looks at the WADA whereabouts system. *International Journal of Sport Policy and Politics, 2*, 255–274.

Walgrave & Koch v. Association Union Cycliste Internationale [1974] Case 36/74 ECR.

Westerholm, R. (July 15, 2014). Mark Emmert salary: NCAA President gets a raise. *University Herald*. Retrieved from http://www.universityherald.com/articles/10419/20140715/mark-emmert-salary-ncaa-president-gets-a-raise-made-1-7m-in-2012-2013-fiscal-year.htm

White, D. V. (1986). Sports violence as criminal assault: Development of the doctrine by Canadian courts. *Duke Law Journal, 6*, 1030–1054.

White Paper on Sport. (2007). Retrieved from http://eur-lex.europa.eu/legal-content/EN/TXT/?uri=CELEX%3A52007DC0391

References

Woodyard, C. (February 7, 2016). Super Bowl ad costs soar—but so does buzz. *USA Today*. Retrieved from http://www.usatoday.com/story/money/2016/02/07/super-bowl-ad-costs-soar----but-so-does-buzz/79903058/

World Anti-Doping Agency. World Anti-Doping Code. Available online at: http://www.wada-ama.org/en/world-anti-doping-program/sports-and-anti-doping-organizations/the-code/

Yang, Y., & Raine, A. (2009). Prefrontal structural and functional brain imaging findings in antisocial, violent, and psychopathic individuals: a meta-analysis. *Psychiatry Research, 174*(2), 81–88.

Yang, J., Peek-Asa, C., Allareddy, V., Phillips, G., Zhang, Y., & Cheng, G. (2007). Patient and hospital characteristics associated with length of stay and hospital charges for pediatric sport-related injury hospitalization in the United States, 2000–2003. *Pediatrics, 19*, 813–820.

Yates, R. A., Yates, R. W., & Bain, P. (2000). *Introduction to law in Canada, 2nd edition*. Scarborough: Prentice-Hall Canada Inc.

Yates, J., & Gillespie, W. (2002). The problem of sports violence and the criminal prosecution solution. *Cornell Journal of Law and Public Policy, 12*, 145–173.

Yesalis, C., & Bahrke, M. (2002). History of doping in sport, In M. Bahrke & C. Yesalis (Eds.), *Performance-enhancing substances in sport and exercise* (pp. v-ix). Champaign, IL: Human Kinetics.

Young, K. (1993). Violence, risk, and liability in male sports culture. *Sociology of Sport Journal, 10*(4), 373–396.

Young, K., & White, P. (2000). Researching sports injury: Reconstructing dangerous masculinities. In J. McKay, M. Messner and D. Sabo (Eds.), *Masculinities, Gender Relations and Sport* (pp. 108–126). Los Angeles: Sage.

Ziegler, E., & Huntley, T. (2013). "It got too tough to not be me": Accommodating transgendered athletes in sport. *Journal of College and University Law 39*, 467–509.

Zillgett, J. (2011). Federal mediator to step into NBA lockout. *USA Today*. Retrieved from http://usatoday30.usatoday.com/sports/basketball/nba/story/2011-10-12/Federal-mediator-to-step-into-NBA-lockout/50745716/1

List of Acronyms

Amateur Athletic Union (AAU)
Alternative Dispute Resolution (ADR)
Amateur Boxing Association of England (ABAE)
Athletics Federation of India (AFI)
Canadian Football League (CFL)
Canadian Soccer Association (CSA)
Collegiate Licensing Company (CLC)
Court of Arbitration for Sport (CAS)
Crown Prosecution Service (CPS)
Dispute Resolution Chamber (DRC)
European Court Reports (ECR)
Electronic Arts (EA)
Entertainment and Sports Programming Network (ESPN)
European Gaming & Betting Association (EGBA)
European Union (EU)
Federal Mediation and Conciliation Service (FMCS)
Fédération Internationale de Football Association (FIFA)
Financial Fair Play (FFP)
German Olympic Sport Association (DOSB)
Grievous Bodily Harm (GBH)
International Association of Athletics Federation (IAAF)
International Biathlon Union (IBU)
International Charter on Physical Education and Sport (ICPES)
International Federation (IF)
International Federation of Football Associations (FIFA)
International Skating Union (ISU)
International Tennis Federation (ITF)
International Olympic Committee (IOC)
Major League Baseball (MLB)
National Basketball Association (NBA)
National Basketball Players Association (NBPA)
National Collegiate Athletics Association (NCAA)
National Federation of State High School Associations (NFHS)
National Football League (NFL)
National Football Players Association (NFPA)
National Hockey League (NHL)
Royal Belgian Football Association (URBSFA)
Treaty on the Functioning of the European Union (TFEU)
UK Athletics Limited (UKA)
UK Central Council of Physical Recreation (CCPR)
Union of European Football Associations (UEFA)
United Nations (UN)
Universal Declaration of Human Rights (UDHR)
Unlawful Internet Gambling Enforcement Act (UIGEA)
Vancouver Committee for the 2010 Olympic and Paralympic Games (VANOC)
World Legal Review (WLR)
World-Anti-Doping Agency (WADA)
World Anti-Doping Code (WADC)
World Chess Federation (FIDE)

Legal Case Index

Attorney General's Reference, 15
Baxter v. IOC, 72–73
Chand v. AFI & IAAF, 24
Decision [2000] Football World Cup, 15
Deliège v. Ligue francophone de judo et disciplines associées ASBL, Ligue belge de judo ASBL, Union européenne de judo, 15
Deutscher Handballbund v Kolpak, 15
Dona v. Mantero, 15
Dunn v. University of Ottawa, 15
Edwards v. BAF and IAAF, 16
Enderby Town FC v. The Football Association, 10
FC Shaktar Donetsk v. Matuzalém Francelino da Silva, Real Zaragoza and FIFA, 93
Garrett v. Canadian Weightlifting Federation, 86, 88
Hart v. Elec. Arts, Inc., 6, 59, 63
Humphrey v. Viacom, Inc., 6, 79–80, 83
In re NCAA Student-Athlete Name & Likeness Litig, 63
Irvine v. Royal Burgess Golfing Society of Edinburgh, 10
Jones v. Welsh Rugby Football Union, 10
Keller v. Elec. Arts, Inc., 6, 59, 63–64
Langone v. Patrick Kaiser & Fanduel, Inc., 6, 80, 83
Lehtonen and others v. Federation Royale Belge de Societies de basketball, 15
Matuzalém v. FIFA and CAS, 93
McInnes v. Onslow-Fane, 85
Meca-Medina & Majcen v. Commission of the European Communities, 16, 31, 74
Miami Dolphins v. Williams, 91
Modahl v. British Athletics Federation Ltd, 71
National Football League Players v. Pro-Football, 91

O'Bannon v. Nat'l Collegiate Athletic Ass'n, 6, 59, 63–64
Ohuruogu v. UK Athletics Limited (UKA) & International Association of Athletics Federations (IAAF), 12
Pechstein v. International Skating Union, 93
People v. Turner, 79
R. v. Barnes, 55–57
R. v. Bertuzzi, 96
R. v. Best, 49
R. v. Bishop, 49
R. v. Billinghurst, 49
R. v. Bowyer, 49
R. v. Bradshaw, 55
R. v. Brown, 50, 52
R. v. Calton, 49
R. v. CC, 56
R. v. Cey, 57
R. v. Collins, 49
R v Coney, 53
R. v. Deverereux, 49
R. v. Evans, 49
R. v. Garfield, 50
R. v. Gingell, 49
R. v. Goodwin, 49
R. v. Hardy, 49
R. v. Henderson, 39
R. v. Johnson, 49
R. v. Lloyd, 42, 49
R. v. Marsh, 49
R. v. McSorley, 14, 55
R. v. Moss, 49
R. v. O'Callaghan, 49–51
R. v. Pepper, 49
R. v. Powell, 49
R. v. Rees, 49
R. v. Unsworth, 49
Reynolds v. IAAF, 71

Sagen v. Vancouver Committee for the 2010 Olympic and Paralympic Games (VANOC), 22
Seattle Times Co. v. Tielsch, 80
Smolden v. Whitworth, 14
Sterling v. Leeds Rugby League Cup, 12
Taylor v. Moorabbin Saints Football League and Football Victoria, 13
Thomas (Next friend of) v. Hamilton Board of Education [1994] O.J. 2444.

Quigley v. UID, 14
URBSFA v. Bosman, 15, 30, 32
Varis v IBU, 71
Vernonia School District 47J v. Acton, 11
Vowles v. Evans, 14
WADA v ITF & Gasquet, 73
Walgrave & Koch v. Association Union Cycliste Internationale, 15